KU-496-680

Contents

★An asterisk next to the name of an organisation in the text indicates that the address can be found in this section

What to Do When Someone Dies

Paul Harris

CONSUMERS' ASSOCIATION

Which? Books are commissioned and researched by
Consumers' Association and published by
Which? Ltd, 2 Marylebone Road, London NW1 4DF
Email address: books@which.net

Distributed by The Penguin Group:
Penguin Books Ltd, 27 Wrights Lane, London W8 5TZ

First edition April 1967
New edition April 1994
Revised editions May 1995, March 1997
Reprinted October 1997, June 1999
Revised editions May 1998, March 2000

Text revised by Paul Harris; Scottish sections supplied by Michael Scanlan and
updated by Diane Campbell and Robert Macaulay; chapter on organ donation
contributed by Hilary Fenton-Harris, Senior Staff Nurse at Poole Hospital Trust
Intensive Care Unit

British Library Cataloguing-in-Publication Data
A catalogue record for this book is available from the British Library

ISBN 0 85202 816 4

For a full list of Which? books, please write to
Which? Books, Castlemead, Gascoyne Way, Hertford X, SG14 1LH
or access our web site at www.which.net

Cover and text design by Kysen Creative Consultants

Typeset by Paston PrePress Ltd, Beccles, Suffolk
Printed and bound in Great Britain by Clays Ltd, St Ives plc

Foreword

We all share two experiences in life: we are all born, and we will all die. While death and bereavement are still subjects from which many shrink, sooner or later someone close to us will die and we will be faced with the responsibility of arranging their funeral. This book shows you how to do this. Since 1967 it has helped many thousands of people, by making it clear what you *must* do (there is not much of this) and describing what you *may* do (of which there is rather a lot more). The book cuts through a morass of confusion, and will make it easier for you to decide on the kind of funeral arrangements that you want, pointing out some of the advantages, disadvantages and difficulties you may encounter in the process.

The book is divided into self-contained chapters, and essential information is duplicated where appropriate to make for easy reference. Essential matters such as obtaining a doctor's certificate and registering a death are clearly explained, and the pros and cons of burial *vs* cremation are outlined. The role of the funeral director, and how to arrange a funeral without the services of a funeral director, is also described, together with the functions of other people with whom you will come into contact: doctors, registrars, clergymen of all denominations, cemetery or crematorium officials, and, in some cases, the police and the coroner. All of these will advise and sometimes instruct, but it is the executor or nearest relative who has the responsibility of making the necessary decisions; *What to Do When Someone Dies* describes what needs to be done, when, and how to set about it.

This book also advises on humanist and other non-Christian funerals. **Chapter 18** examines briefly the personal aspects of death and bereavement, and **Chapter 4** provides relevant details about organ donation and making provision to leave a body for medical research. There is also a guide to Social Security benefits which may be obtained from the Benefits Agency, including help from the Social Fund towards paying for the funeral (see **Chapter 21**). Prices are quoted wherever possible, but as many of these change annually, or even more frequently they should be checked carefully in the local area. This is particularly true of state benefits.

New developments

Several years ago, we commented that our society appeared to be polarising between those who broadly see a funeral as a necessary means of disposing of a body quickly and cheaply and those for whom a funeral is a grand celebration of a person's life, to be accorded time and expense. This trend appears to be increasing, but the majority of people still fall between these two extremes, wanting to accord their relatives and friends due dignity and respect, but not wishing to pay more than is necessary.

Two areas in which interest has increased substantially are pre-paid funeral plans and do-it-yourself funerals: brief advice is given in both areas.

An increasing number of people are setting up web sites in memory of relatives and friends. This can offer an informal way of remembering someone and provide much information to those with access to the Internet (see **Chapter 16**).

There has been considerable development in woodland burial grounds, which now exist within reasonable reach of most towns and cities. In these, burial takes place as normal, but memorials are usually limited to a tree or a shrub (see **Chapter 9**).

Funeral supermarkets are no longer the novelty they were a few years ago. In most major cities, all the items required for a funeral may be examined, from a simple cardboard coffin to elaborate American-style caskets and expensive memorial masonry, in one retail outlet. All such premises have staff who will give advice, and some have been trained to make all the necessary funeral arrangements. Caution should be exercised in selecting items to ensure that those chosen are really wanted, always bearing in mind that disbursements (the cost of burial or cremation, minister's fees etc.) must be added to the cost.

The funeral industry

The funeral industry has changed considerably in recent decades. Many small, independent businesses – and some large ones – have sold out to groups or corporations. The Co-operative Funeral Service is the largest, supplying about 25 per cent of the funerals in the UK, followed by SCI, which supplies about 13 per cent. It is common practice for the original trading names to be retained when the business has been sold to a conglomerate; however, all SCI branches are required to display their ownership prominently. Concerns have been expressed over the marketing techniques of some companies, and, as in any buying situation, consumers should not allow themselves to be pressurised into buying something that they do not really want or cannot afford (particularly when considering memorials and pre-paid funeral plans).

Most funeral directors are members of the National Association of Funeral Directors (NAFD), the Society of Allied and Independent Funeral Directors (SAIF) or the Funeral Standards Council (FSC). If you are arranging a funeral, try to select a funeral director who is registered with one of these organisations to ensure that your rights are protected. The FSC has recently emerged as the largest of the associations, with the various co-operative societies, SCI and smaller groups and independents in membership. FSC and SAIF members are involved in the Funeral Ombudsman Scheme, which settles disputes between the public and FSC-associated funeral directors. The Ombudsman scheme is associated with, but independent of, the FSC: SAIF is not a member of the FSC. The NAFD, FSC and SAIF all have their codes of practice designed to regulate the service and protect the client.

However, at the moment funeral directors need no qualifications and have no system of registration: almost anyone can set up a business and start trading. The government, Consumers' Association and many funeral directors – including the author of this book – feel strongly that funeral directors need to be trained and qualified, and that some form of registration is imperative. People are at their most vulnerable at times of bereavement. Regulation of the funeral profession would help to ensure the provision of a professional and caring service, and that no advantage is taken of people in their distress. The Office of Fair Trading is currently conducting an investigation into the 'at need' (compared with 'pre-need') funeral service which will, it is hoped, lead to registration; no findings have been published at the time of going to press.

Although it is impossible within the confines of this book to explore all the details of every relevant area, the list of addresses attached at the end of the book will lead you to organisations from which further information can be obtained.

Chapter 1

Death

You may discover someone apparently dead, and it can be difficult to tell whether he or she really is dead or not. For instance, someone rescued from water may appear not to breathe, yet might be revived by artificial respiration or the 'kiss of life'.

The body temperature drops at the rate of one or two degrees centigrade an hour for the first few hours after death, so someone who has been dead for an hour or so is appreciably colder than normal. The extremities – feet and hands – get cold first. But very low body temperature alone is not a sure sign of death because comatose or unconscious people can also seem abnormally cold.

If there is any doubt whether someone is dead, treat him or her as being still alive.

Telling the doctor

The first thing to do is to call the doctor. If you do not know how or where to get hold of a doctor, dial 999 for the emergency ambulance service. If there is any doubt at all as to whether the person has actually died, call the doctor immediately. However, if the doctor has been in regular attendance and the person concerned has been expected to die, there is no need to disturb the doctor in the middle of the night: early the next morning will be sufficient.

Ask whether the doctor is going to come. If the death has been peaceful and expected, the doctor may not feel it necessary to come, or at least not straight away. If the doctor does not intend coming, ask his or her permission for a funeral director to remove the body, which may not be done otherwise. If a decision has already been made that the funeral will involve cremation, you should tell the doctor at this point as papers will need to be prepared which will involve the doctor in examining the body and arranging for another doctor to perform a similar examination. Some doctors make a point of seeing the body of every patient who has died as soon as is convenient. However, the doctor may prefer to examine the deceased at the funeral director's mortuary, in which case (with the doctor's permission) the body may be removed by the appropriate funeral director. If the body is to be kept at home, keep the relevant room as cool as possible by turning off the room heating, keeping the door closed, and, if necessary, leaving a window open. In hot weather it may be advisable to keep the body cool by using cloth-wrapped ice packs.

Laying out the body

The initial preparation of the body for burial or cremation is called **laying out**; if this is done by a nurse or in hospital it will be referred to as 'last offices', while a funeral director will refer to it as 'first offices' (because it is the last service performed for the deceased by the medical profession and the first by the funeral director). This involves washing and tidying the body, closing the eyelids and ensuring that the jaw remains closed. The hair is tidied and sometimes washed, the arms and legs are straightened and, if necessary, the body's orifices are stopped with cotton wool. A man may need to be shaved as the hair continues to grow for some time after death. If laying out is done by a funeral director, the body will be dressed ready for the funeral, either in a funeral gown or, if preferred by the relatives, in everyday clothes.

There is a small but growing tendency for the family to arrange and conduct funerals for deceased relatives – see 'Arranging a funeral without a funeral director', **Chapter 15**. In this case, you can do the laying out yourself at home. Most people still prefer to hand over funeral arrangements to a funeral director, who will then attend to the laying out. This may be done at home, if preferred; a funeral director will not normally charge extra for this service within working hours, but will usually prefer to attend to the deceased at his or her mortuary. Many hospitals now provide only a basic laying out service, leaving the majority to be done by the funeral director.

Rigor mortis is a stiffening of the muscles, which usually begins within about six hours after death and gradually extends over the whole body in about 24 hours; after this it usually begins to wear off. Rigor mortis is less pronounced in the body of an elderly person.

When someone has been dead for half an hour or more, parts of the skin often begin to discolour with purple/black patches. This is called **hypostasis**, or post mortem staining, and is due to blood settling in the body due to the action of gravity.

If someone has died at home in bed, quietly and expectedly, it is perfectly in order to rearrange the body and tidy the room. If, however, someone collapses and dies unexpectedly, or a dead body is discovered in unusual circumstances, you must summon the doctor immediately and do as little as possible until he or she comes. Do not move the body unless there are exceptional circumstances, for example, if someone collapses and dies while crossing a road or at the top of a flight of stairs.

Calling the police

If you think that death appears to have been caused by an accident or violence, or to have occurred in other non-natural or suspicious circumstances, you must inform the police at once. The police will inform the coroner.

Do not touch or move anything in the room, or allow anyone else to do so, until the police say that you may. The police will almost certainly want to take statements from anyone who was with the deceased when he or she died, or who discovered the body, but no one is obliged to give a statement to the police. If there is an inquest later, anyone who has made a statement may be called as a witness, as may any person whom the coroner believes may be able to give information about the death.

If a body cannot be identified immediately, the police circulate a description in police journals, and occasionally to the general press, too. Anyone who might be able to identify the body usually has to go to the mortuary with the police.

If the police are called and no relative or other person responsible is immediately available, the police take possession of any cash or valuables. As a general rule, this property is given up to whomever can later prove the right to it. The police also take away any article which may have a bearing on the cause of death – a letter or bottle of pills, for example – in case this is needed by the coroner.

Medical certificate of the cause of death

Every death that occurs in the UK must be registered at the local registrar's office within five days (see **Chapter 2**) and the registrar will require a certificate providing medical evidence of the cause of death. Normally, the doctor who has been attending the deceased will sign the certificate, but he or she cannot do so if there is any doubt whatsoever about the actual cause of death.

If the doctor knows the cause of death, he or she will provide the relatives with a certificate which states (to the best of the doctor's knowledge) the cause or causes of death, the last date on which he or she saw the patient alive and whether or not a doctor has seen the body since death occurred. This will usually be given to the family in a sealed envelope, together with a small form which gives basic details about registering the death. No charge is made for the certificate.

If the doctor is uncertain for any reason about the actual cause of death or has not seen the patient within a period of 14 days before death occurred, he or she cannot sign the death certificate. In such cases the coroner must be informed (see **Chapter 6**) – the coroner's officer will normally contact the family and explain procedures. The body will then be taken to the coroner's mortuary (usually at a local hospital) where the cause of death will be investigated, which may or may not involve a post mortem examination. In such cases, the period for registration may be extended as long as the registrar is informed of the circumstances so that appropriate action can be taken. The relatives arranging the funeral should do this.

In normal cases where the doctor signs the medical certificate of the cause of death, this must be used to register the death at the register office in the district or sub-district in which the death occurred. However, in England and Wales information may be given at any other register office, if this is more convenient. This will then be passed on to the register office in the sub-district where the death occurred (see **Chapter 2**, 'Registering the Death').

Chapter 2

Registering the death

In England, Wales and Northern Ireland, a death should be registered within five days of its happening. Registration can be delayed for a further nine days provided the registrar receives, in writing, confirmation that a medical certificate of the cause of death has been signed by the doctor.

Under English law, all deaths must be registered in the registration sub-district in which they took place or in which the body was found. Should it be more convenient, however, information regarding the registration (see below) may be taken to any register office in England and Wales (*not* Scotland or Northern Ireland) – the 'attesting registrar' – from which it will be passed on to the relevant register office.

The medical certificate of the cause of death must be presented at the register office in the sub-district where the death occurred (the receiving registrar). Following registration the necessary documents will be returned, normally to the informant, by first-class post. The informant must decide how many copies of the death certificate will be required, and pay for them (normally by cheque – credit cards may not be accepted) when giving the information to the attesting registrar. If the informant requires the death certificate(s) to be sent to someone else, he or she must give the name and address to the attesting registrar.

This will obviously delay the receipt of such documents; sometimes it is possible for the green certificate, authorising burial or cremation, to be sent directly to, or be collected by, the funeral director carrying out the funeral arrangements. The rest of the documents will then be sent to the informant, or to whatever other addresses the informant has indicated.

A list of names, addresses and telephone numbers of local registrars of births and deaths is usually displayed in doctors' surgeries and in public libraries and other public buildings, together with their office hours and a description of the sub-district they cover.

Usually, whoever is giving the information goes in person to the registrar's office. An increasing number of registration districts now operate on an appointments system, although it is usually possible for you just to go along during the registrar's office hours and wait until he or she is free to see you.

The informant

When a medical certificate of the cause of death is completed by a doctor, he or she must also complete that part of it which provides information for the informant or person informing the registrar of the details of the death which has occurred.

One side of the form is entitled 'notice to informant' and provides details of the information which the registrar will require:

- the date and place of death
- the full name and surname of the deceased (and the maiden name if the deceased was a married woman)
- the date and place of birth of the deceased
- the occupation of the deceased (and husband's name and occupation if the deceased was a married woman or widow)
- the usual address of the deceased
- whether the deceased was in receipt of a pension or allowance from public funds
- if the deceased was married, the date of birth of the surviving partner.

The form also states that the deceased's medical card should be taken and given to the registrar. However, if it cannot be found, registration should not be delayed: the card may be supplied to the registrar on a later occasion.

The other side of the form provides details of those who are qualified to act as informants. If the death has occurred inside a house or public building, any of the following may register the death:

- a relative of the deceased who was present at the death
- a relative of the deceased who was present during the last illness
- a relative of the deceased who was not present at the death or during the last illness but who lives in the district or sub-district where the death occurred

- a person who is not a relative but who was present at the time of death
- the occupier (e.g. the matron of a nursing home or warden of pensioners' flats) of the building where the death occurred, if he or she was aware of the details of the death
- any inmate of the building where the death occurred, if he or she was aware of the details of the death
- the person causing the disposal of the body (this means the person accepting the responsibility for arranging the funeral – *not* the funeral director, who is not allowed to register the death).

These categories of informants are given in order of precedence.

If the person has been found dead elsewhere, the following are qualified to register the death:

- any relative of the deceased able to provide the registrar with the required details
- any person present at the time of death
- the person who found the body
- the person in charge of the body (which will be the police if the body cannot be identified)
- the person accepting responsibility for arranging the funeral.

The responsibility for registering the death cannot be delegated to a person who is not qualified under the law to act as informant: should such a person attend the register office, the registrar will refuse to register the death and will require a qualified informant to attend. If the doctor is sending the medical certificate of cause of death direct to the registrar, sufficient time for the certificate to be delivered must be allowed before going to register the death.

If the registrar finds that the information the doctor has given on the medical certificate of cause of death is inadequate or that the death was due to some cause that should have been reported to the coroner, he or she must inform the coroner accordingly and await written clearance before proceeding with the registration. He or she must also inform the coroner if it is found that the doctor had not seen the deceased within 14 days prior to death or after death. In cases where a coroner's inquest has been held, the coroner will act as the informant and provide the registrar with all the necessary details; in this case there is no need for the family and relatives to register the death, although they will need to attend the register office if copies of the death certificate are needed. The table on page 20 summarises the documents required, and the chart on page 49 outlines the typical procedure following a death.

Procedure

The procedure for registering a death is a simple question-and-answer interview between the registrar and the informant.

The registrar will, first of all, make sure that the death took place in his or her sub-district; a death cannot be registered if it occurred in any place outside the registrar's sub-district. He or she will ask in what capacity whoever is registering the death qualifies to be the informant – relative, present at the death, or other reason. The registrar may ask if the informant has brought the deceased's birth certificate and marriage certificate, and National Health Service medical card. It is not essential for the informant to have these, but they contain some of the information the registrar will need.

Then the registrar fills in a draft form for the register of deaths with the date of death and exactly where it occurred, the sex, names and surname of the dead person. It is as well to give all the names by which the deceased has ever been known, so that there can be no doubt as to whom the particulars refer. In order to avoid difficulties over identity in connection with probate, insurance policies, pensions and bank accounts, the names should be the same as those on birth and marriage certificates, and on any other relevant documents. The maiden surname of a married woman is required. The date and place of birth of the dead person, and last address, are entered. For someone who died away from home, the home address should be given.

Next, the registrar will want to know the last full-time occupation of the deceased, and whether he or she was retired at the time of death. A woman who was married or widowed at the time of her death would be described as 'wife of' or 'widow of', followed by the name and occupation of her husband, in addition to her own occupation or profession. A woman who had never been married or a woman whose marriage had been dissolved would have her occupation recorded, with no reference to her marital status.

Children under the age of 16 are described as 'son of' or 'daughter of', followed by the names and occupations of the parents.

The registrar copies the medical cause of death from the doctor's certificate or the coroner's notification, and adds the name and qualification of the doctor or coroner.

On the draft form, but not in the register itself, the registrar enters the deceased's National Health Service number. If the deceased was over 16 years old, additional information is requested: marital status at the time of death (single, married, widowed or divorced) and the date of birth of any widow or widower left. This information is not entered in the register in England and Wales, and is used only for the preparation of population statistics by the Registrar General.

The registrar will ask for the deceased's medical card. This is to enable the National Health Service register to be kept up to date.

Entry in the register

Many register offices are now computerised; it is likely that your information about the deceased will be entered into a computer system and your copy, or copies, of the death certificate produced by a computer printer. Do not be surprised by this, but note that you will still be required to sign the register in the usual way.

The informant should check the draft of the proposed entry in the register to make sure that there is nothing wrong or misleading in it. When the particulars are agreed, the registrar makes the entry in the register itself and asks the informant to check and sign it. The informant should sign his or her usual signature, even if this is not his or her whole name. The registrar has to use special ink for the register, so sign with the pen offered.

After adding the date of the registration, the registrar signs the entry in the final space. Any errors can be corrected without formality before the entry has been signed, but once it is signed by the registrar, the entry cannot be corrected without the authority of the Registrar General, who may require documentary evidence to justify the correction. The registrar can now let you have copies of the entry in the register (the death certificates) which you may need for probate and other purposes. In addition to the copies of the death certificate, the registrar will provide, without charge, a copy of a form for Social Security purposes, and a green certificate for the funeral director, authorising him or her to carry out the funeral.

Make a note of the number of the entry in the register and the date, and also note the registration district, because you may need more copies of the entry later. Copies of entries in the current register cost £3.50 (1999/2000), increasing to £6.50 after about one month, once the register is in the custody of the Superintendent Registrar. If, subsequently, details of the registration and registration district are lost, application for a search must be made to the Public Search Room,★ and the fee for a copy of the entry made in this way is £11 (1999/2000).

Documents for registration

Document	Source	Function	Recipient
notice to informant	doctor	gives details of who must register death and what particulars will be required	via relative to registrar
medical certificate of cause of death	doctor	states cause of death	to registrar (direct or via relative)
If coroner involved:			
coroner's notification	coroner	confirms or gives details of cause of death	to registrar (direct or via relative)
or			
coroner's certificate after inquest	coroner	gives all the particulars required for death to be registered	direct to registrar

Registering a stillbirth

In the case of a stillbirth both birth and death need to be registered, a single operation which has to be done within 42 days.

People qualified to register a stillbirth are (as for live births): the mother; the father if the child would have been legitimate had it been born alive; the occupier of the house or other premises in which the stillbirth occurred; a person who was present at the stillbirth or who found the stillborn child.

A stillborn child is a child born after the 24th week of pregnancy which did not at any time after being completely delivered from its mother breathe or show any other signs of life.

If a doctor was in attendance at a stillbirth or examined the body of the stillborn child, he or she can issue a certificate of stillbirth, stating the cause of stillbirth and the duration of the pregnancy. A certified midwife can also issue the certificate if no doctor was there. If no doctor or midwife was in attendance at, or after, the birth, one of the parents, or some other qualified informant, can make a declaration on a form (**Form 35**, available from the registrar of births and deaths), saying that to the best of his or her knowledge and belief the child was stillborn.

If there is any doubt whether the child was born alive or not, the case must be reported to the coroner of the district, who may then order a post mortem or an inquest and will issue a certificate of the cause of death when the inquiries are complete.

When registering a stillbirth, the registrar has to have the doctor's or midwife's certificate, or a declaration of the stillbirth. Whoever goes to register has to tell the registrar of the name of the child where given, the name, surname and maiden name of the mother, her place of birth and her usual residence at the time of the child's birth; if she had never been married, her occupation is also required. If the child would have been legitimate, the name, surname and occupation of the father and his place of birth are required.

If the parents are not married at the time of their baby's birth but do still want the father's details entered, they should ask the registrar to guide them through the rather more involved procedures.

If the father and mother are married to each other, the registrar asks the month and year of the marriage, and the number of the mother's previous children, both born alive and stillborn, by her present and any former husband; this information is needed for statistical purposes only in order to forecast population trends and is not entered in the register.

A certified copy of the stillbirth entry (death certificate) is now obtainable, costing £3.50, although a certificate of registration will be provided free of charge to the informant if it is requested.

Loss of the foetus before the 24th week does not fall within the legal definition of a stillbirth and is usually considered a miscarriage. If the mother was in hospital at the time, the hospital may offer to arrange for the disposal of the remains. But if the parent(s) would like these to be buried or cremated in the usual way, it should be possible to arrange this with a local cemetery or crematorium, provided a form of medical certificate is completed.

Most crematoria make minimal charges for the funerals of stillborn or miscarried children and many funeral directors will provide their services on such occasions free of charge. This means that they will probably not charge for their professional services but will be obliged to pass on any fees for crematoria etc. that they may incur on behalf of their clients. Some hospitals now offer 'reverent disposal' of stillborn and miscarried children, which often involves a simple ceremony led by the hospital chaplain. It should be noted that in such cases there may be no ashes produced for subsequent burial or scattering. See also **Chapter 19**.

Chapter 3

Death in hospital

The Centre for Policy on Ageing produced a study in 1983 which found that 70 per cent of deaths in urban areas at that time took place in hospital: the percentage has since increased considerably. When someone has died in a hospital or similar institution, what happens up to the time of registration is slightly different from the way that arrangements are made if the death occurred at home.

The relatives, or whoever was named as next of kin when the patient was admitted, are informed of the death by the ward nursing staff. If death was unexpected, the result of an accident, or occurred during an operation or while the patient was recovering from an anaesthetic, the coroner will be involved. Normally, all deaths occurring within 24 hours of an operation or admission to hospital will be reported to the coroner. This so-called '24-hour admissions rule' is not a statutory requirement, but many coroners require such referrals as a matter of course, with a view to ensuring that a death which may be due to unnatural causes is not missed.

If the coroner is of the opinion that a post mortem examination may prove an inquest to be unnecessary, he or she may arrange for a post mortem to be held (Section 19(1) of the Coroner's Act 1988). The coroner has a statutory right to order a post mortem examination whenever a death has been reported to him or her.

Deaths which occur under suspicious circumstances, or are due to medical mishaps, industrial disease, violence, neglect, abortion, or any kind of poisoning must, by law, be reported to the coroner. If the person who died was not already an in-patient at the hospital, a member of the family may be asked to identify the body.

Hospitals differ from each other in procedure, but it is usually the administrative rather than the medical staff who make the necessary arrangements with the relatives. When the coroner is involved, it will not be possible to issue a medical certificate of the cause of death (see

Chapter 6), but in normal cases this is usually completed by a hospital doctor and given to the next of kin. If the person died before a hospital doctor had a chance to diagnose the cause, then the deceased patient's own doctor may be asked to issue the medical certificate. If the GP feels that there is reasonable doubt as to the cause of death, he or she will be unable to sign the certificate, and this too will be reported to the coroner. Once the coroner becomes involved, the responsibility for the body lies with the coroner's office rather than the hospital. The coroner, through his or her officer, will provide relatives with the necessary information; the hospital will tell the relatives how to contact the coroner's office.

All hospitals have considerable experience of dealing with bereaved relatives, and the staff appointed to this duty are usually patient and sympathetic. However, demands on time are considerable, emergencies often arise, and it is inevitable that, from time to time, some waiting will be involved. The hospital will make its procedures clear, but if death occurs in the evening or the middle of the night, an appointment will be made to deal with the formalities on the following day. The deceased's possessions will have to be removed from the hospital; these are normally available from the hospital's property office, for collection only by the next of kin or his or her authorised representative. A signature will be required.

If the medical certificate of the cause of death can be issued at the hospital, the relatives of the deceased have to arrange for the body to be removed from the hospital mortuary. This is normally the responsibility of the funeral director (but see **Chapter 15**). The hospital will not recommend any particular funeral director, but can sometimes provide a list of names and addresses of funeral directors in the local area. The funeral director concerned should be informed of the situation promptly; most operate a 24-hour emergency service, but there is no need to inform him or her of a hospital death occurring in the middle of the night until next morning. The next of kin or executor will normally have to sign a form authorising the removal of the body to the funeral director's premises. If the funeral is to involve cremation, the necessary medical forms will be completed at the hospital; the body cannot be removed until this is done, and will sometimes involve a delay of up to 48 hours – longer if a weekend is included. There is a charge for these forms; this is usually paid by the funeral director, and the amount added to the funeral account.

Post mortem

Hospitals sometimes want to carry out a post mortem examination, or autopsy, to find out more about the cause of death. This 'hospital post mortem' does not involve the coroner and cannot be undertaken without the permission of the next of kin: the next of kin, or executor, should therefore be prepared to give a response to this question when visiting the hospital after death has occurred. In cases where the coroner *is* involved, permission for a post mortem is not required: should the coroner order a post mortem, the law requires that it must take place. Relatives will not automatically be told the results of a post mortem, and should ask for the results if they want to know. Under some circumstances, relatives may be asked if they have any objection to the use of the deceased's organs for transplant surgery. Even if the patient had completed a donor card and enrolled on the NHS Organ Donor Register,* the relatives will be consulted before any organs are removed (see **Chapter 4**).

Registration

The procedure for registering a death in hospital is the same as for a death that occurred at home, but the death must be registered at the register office in the registration district where the hospital is situated. However, if that same registration district or sub-district has another office, or out-station, which is nearer and therefore more convenient for the relatives, registration may be carried out there. Furthermore, information regarding the registration may be given at any register office in England and Wales (please see **Chapter 2**, 'Registration'). For deaths which took place in Scotland, please see **Chapter 7**.

Funeral arrangements

Where there are no relatives or friends to arrange and pay for the funeral, the health authority can do so. Hospitals have arrangements with local funeral directors to provide a simple funeral. Although, technically, the health authority is responsible, in practice, the funeral arrangements are made by the staff of the hospital where the patient died.

Chapter 4

Organ donation for transplantation

Organ transplantation is one of the greatest medical success stories of our time. Its effectiveness, however, is severely limited because the demand for organs far exceeds their availability. During the last 50 years, it has become possible to transplant many types of body tissue, from skin to major organs. Kidney, liver, heart and heart-lung transplants have now become routine operations, and the process is constantly being refined and developed. The technique of human organ transplantation currently allows more than 5,400 people not only to survive (1998 figures), but to achieve a fuller and healthier lifestyle. In addition, a further 3,700 have their eyesight restored annually through corneal transplants. For each person so treated, several must be turned away. When thought is being given to future funeral arrangements, serious consideration should therefore be given to the possibility of becoming an organ donor.

Brain stem death

If the body of a potential donor were to be left until the traditional signs of death were apparent (lack of pulse, coldness, rigor mortis and so on), the organs would have deteriorated through lack of oxygen, and would no longer be of any use. The relevant organs must clearly be removed as soon as possible after death has occurred.

No organ can be removed for transplantation until the patient concerned is diagnosed as being 'brain stem dead'. This occurs when the part of the brain responsible for maintaining the essential functions of the body is irreversibly damaged. This may be caused by head injury, cerebral haemorrhage, primary brain tumour, or conditions where the brain has been seriously deprived of oxygen. Such patients will normally be in hospital, with life functions maintained on a ventilator. In order to determine brain stem death, the cranial nerves are tested by a stringent set of tests laid down in the Code of Practice of the Conference of Royal Medical Colleges, revised in March 1998. The lack of the following signs signifies absence of life in the brain stem:

- the pupils of the eye do not respond to light
- blinking does not occur when the cornea of the eye is touched
- there are no eye movements when the ears are irrigated with ice-cold water
- there is no gag or cough reflex
- there is no response to painful stimuli.

If all these reflexes are found to be absent, the patient's ventilator is briefly disconnected to see if the patient makes any attempt to breathe unaided. Examination is carried out by two doctors, competent in this field, who have been registered for more than five years and are not members of the transplant team. At least one must be a consultant. When both sets of tests confirm brain stem death, the person is declared to be dead, and the legal time of death is given as the time when the first set of tests were completed.

A patient must be under 75 for his or her major organs to be suitable for transplantation; he or she must have suffered complete and irreversible brain stem damage, normally be maintained on a hospital ventilator, and have no malignancy other than non-aggressive primary brain tumour. The patient must be HIV-negative, and be free from major infection and the hepatitis B and hepatitis C viruses. He or she must also be of a compatible blood group and tissue-type to the planned recipient.

In order to provide healthy organs for transplantation, the body must receive a continuous supply of oxygen, which will continue to be artificially provided by a ventilator until the organs concerned are removed in the operating theatre by the transplant team. The donor patient will therefore appear a natural colour, the heart will continue to beat, and breathing will be maintained by the ventilator. In spite of this, the patient will be dead, totally unable to perceive or feel anything at all. Families who wish to see their relatives after organs have been removed for transplantation are normally encouraged to do so.

Organs for transplantation

There are specific criteria for the donation of different organs, but basically the organs concerned must be in good working order; obviously, diseased kidneys would be unsuitable, as would the lungs of a person who had smoked heavily.

The following organs are those most commonly used for transplantation:

The kidney

Each year over 2,500 patients in the UK develop chronic renal failure; kidney transplantation saves many lives, and leads to a greatly improved quality of life for many more. Further, a transplant frees dialysis space (a 'kidney machine') for another patient. Kidneys are viable for 48 hours after retrieval from the donor; the maximum donor age is 75. The source of kidneys for transplantation is normally from hospital patients maintained on ventilators following brain stem death, but under certain circumstances kidneys can be retrieved from donors in other situations within 40 minutes of death.

The liver

Liver transplants are required for patients with a congenital malformation of the liver, chronic liver disease, hepatic failure, some cases of cancer of the liver, and inborn metabolic errors. Liver transplants for such have been successfully carried out in the UK since 1968.

The heart

The first heart transplant in the UK was carried out in 1979 at Papworth Hospital: heart transplantation is now considered for patients with severe cardiac failure who are considered unsuitable for heart surgery, and who have a decreased life expectancy.

The heart and lung

The first heart and lung transplant in the UK took place in 1985. This operation is now carried out for people with conditions leading to advanced primary lung disease, or lung disease occurring as a result of cardiac problems or cystic fibrosis.

The lungs
One or both lungs may be transplanted.

The pancreas
Transplantation of the pancreas is a recent development, and is used in some patients with type 1 diabetes. The pancreas may be transplanted by itself, or together with the kidneys; both are transplanted when the patient has diabetes together with renal failure.

Heart valves (tissues)
These may be transplanted following removal from a donor up to 48 hours after death. Usage is mainly for children with congenital heart defects.

The cornea (tissues)
Corneal damage is a major cause of blindness, but thousands have now had their sight restored by corneal grafting. There is no age limit for corneal donation, and the process has an excellent success rate. The need to wear spectacles does not usually affect the suitability of the donor. Corneas can be removed up to 24 hours after the heart has stopped beating; the patient does not need to be maintained on a hospital ventilator. Corneas can be retrieved from patients who have died in many different circumstances; the 1968 Corneal Tissues Act now allows qualified technicians to remove corneal tissue – as there are more technicians than surgeons, a greater number of donated corneas can now be retrieved.

Relatives of patients not dying in hospital who want to carry out their wishes regarding corneal donation should first of all consult the donor's GP and/or the ophthalmic department of the local hospital. In all cases, action must be taken as quickly as possible; at any rate, within 12 hours of death. A special Corneal Transplant Service (run by the Department of Health as part of the UK transplant service, with contributory funding from the Iris Fund for Prevention of Blindness★) takes corneas from donors to the nearest hospital grafting centre or eye bank with minimal delay.

Other transplants
Other parts of the body which can be transplanted include skin, bone, joints, connective tissue, major blood vessels, fetal cells and bone marrow.

Religious and cultural issues

Decisions to donate organs from the deceased may be complicated by religious and cultural influences. The extent and interpretation of these influences will probably vary from family to family, but the basic outline following will apply in most situations.

Buddhists do not generally object to organ donation, as helping others is a fundamental belief.

Christians: organ donation and transplantation is usually considered acceptable to Roman Catholics and most Protestants, although some Protestant sects are strongly opposed.

Christian Scientists object to all forms of organ donation and transplantation.

Hindus and Sikhs have no objections to organ donation, although reservations regarding post mortem operations are frequently expressed.

Jehovah's Witnesses are advised by the Watchtower Society that organ donation and acceptance for transplantation is a matter for individual choice.

Jews generally raise no objection in principle to organ donation, since the prohibitive aspect of Jewish Law can be overridden in order to save life. However, the Law insists that the success of the transplant procedure must be well established, and that no vital organs may be removed until death is confirmed by the complete cessation of all spontaneous life functions. Some Orthodox Jews object to all forms of organ donation and transplantation.

Mormons: the Church of Jesus Christ of the Latter Day Saints expresses no objection to organ donation.

Muslims are subject to Islamic Law, which states that the body must be buried as soon as possible after death. Together with reluctance to permit any interference with the dead, this tends to prohibit organ donation. However, the Muslim Law (Shariah) Council UK issued a directive in 1955 supporting organ donation and transplantation.

NHS Organ Donor Register

This register has been set up as a computer database at the UK Transplant Support Service Authority (UKTSSA). The register is accessible to all transplant co-ordinators, and can be checked each time a potential donor becomes available.

Relatives of donors are still asked to consent to donation, but with an individual's name included on the register and a donor card being carried, the decision is made easier for everyone. Any driving licence issued after March 1993 may be marked in the box on the back to indicate a readiness to donate organs after death, and applicants for new driving licences may indicate to the DVLA★ at Swansea that their wishes to be entered on the NHS Organ Donor Register be printed on the licence. Otherwise, those wishing to register may do so by post, or using one of the special forms available from doctors, chemists, hospitals, libraries and many public places. Alternatively, they may contact the NHS Organ Donor Registration Service.★ It remains very important that family and friends should be informed of an individual's wishes. Advice about how to notify the relevant people and organisations is given on page 162. A leaflet entitled *Questions and Answers on the Organ Donor Register* is available free of charge from the NHS Organ Donor Register.★ It answers common queries people have about organ donation. Further information may be obtained by contacting UKTSSA.★

Legal aspects of organ donation

Transplantation in Britain is governed by three items of legislation: the Human Tissues Act 1961, the Corneal Tissue Act 1986 and the Human Organs Transplants Act 1989; the first two relate to organ donation following death, while the third relates to living donors.

Removal of organs can be authorised if the deceased has made a declaration in writing (usually in a will, by informing the NHS Organ Donor Register, and/or by carrying a donor card), or an oral declaration in the presence of two witnesses that his or her organs may be so used. Alternatively, organs may be removed if, after making reasonable enquiry, there is no reason to believe that the deceased had objected to organ donation, and surviving relatives do not object. Authorisation is given by the person lawfully in possession of the body; this could be a close relative, the person owning the house where the patient died (or hospital administrator), or, in the case of a post mortem or inquest, the coroner. The law supports the view that the hospital authority is legally in possession of the body of a deceased patient until it is 'claimed'.

In any case where it is unclear whether death is due to natural causes, the coroner must be consulted in order to gain consent for organ or tissue donation. This will normally be the responsibility of the hospital consultant, and not a matter for friends or family. The coroner has the power to refuse consent to the removal of organs for transplantation if he or she feels that this may adversely affect any investigation in progress.

The practice of 'elective ventilation' (artificially ventilating a patient before death has been diagnosed solely to obtain organs later) is unlawful in the UK.

BODY

The British Organ Donors Society, or BODY,★ is a voluntary organisation and charitable trust formed in 1984 to help and support donor and recipient families, and to promote organ donation and transplantation.

Body donated for medical education or research

A number of people express the wish that their body should be used after death for medical research. Bodies donated in this way are used by doctors and medical students who are studying and researching the structure and function of the normal human body. (Research into specific medical diseases is not carried out in these examinations.) If such a wish was expressed by the deceased, the next of kin or executor should immediately telephone HM Inspector of Anatomy★ for details of the relevant anatomy school.

Medical schools are, in fact, offered far more bodies than can possibly be accepted and it should be recognised that the offering or willing of a body to medical research does not necessarily mean that it will be accepted. Or, at the time of death there may be some specific reason why the body cannot be accepted: for instance, if the coroner is involved, if death has occurred as the result of certain illnesses, or if death occurs too far away for the relevant medical school to transport the body practically. Until acceptance of the body is confirmed, the family should continue to make arrangements for the funeral in case the body is not accepted.

33

Arrangements prior to death

If a body is to be accepted for medical research, it is imperative that arrangements are made with a specific medical school well before death occurs; specific forms must be completed in advance and should be left with the family, bank or solicitor along with instructions for immediate action when death occurs. If the body is accepted, arrangements will be made by the medical school for it to be collected straight away by a contracted funeral director and taken to the school. In the meantime, the next of kin or executor should obtain the medical certificate of the cause of death from the doctor in charge of the case and register the death as soon as possible. The registrar's green certificate for burial or cremation (see page 38) should also be sent to the medical school.

Donation of the brain for research

The Parkinson's Disease Society* Brain Research Centre, which is part of the Institute of Neurology at University College, London, has a unique collection of tissue donated by individuals who died either from Parkinson's disease or a related disorder. Brain donation by people with no neurological disease is also important, in order that 'control' tissue for comparison may be available. Brain tissue is used to study the effects of disease; tissue is also supplied for additional research projects throughout the UK and internationally.

Brain donation is a separate issue from other organ donation, and cannot be included on the NHS Organ Donor Register. Those indicating to the Register that all their organs may be used will not be considered for brain donation unless the Parkinson's Disease Society has been instructed to that effect. Potential donors must notify the Society of their intentions in advance, or leave clear instructions that this should be done in the event of their death.

Funeral arrangements

It is the responsibility of the medical school to arrange and pay for burial or cremation when the appropriate time comes. The family and executors need make no further arrangements: burial or cremation will be provided according to the wishes of the deceased and next of kin. If the body is eventually to be cremated, the executor may be asked to complete and sign the statutory application form for cremation, **Form A**; however, this may also be signed by the professor of the medical school.

The medical school will pay all expenses for a simple funeral, unless the relatives ask to be allowed to make their own arrangements, at which point the body will be given back and the funeral expenses will become the responsibility of the family. If the medical school makes the funeral arrangements, a simple ceremony will be conducted by a minister or priest of the faith professed by the deceased, unless otherwise requested. The medical school does not put up individual headstones.

If the relatives of the deceased do not wish to make funeral arrangements themselves, but ask for burial or cremation in some place other than that normally used by the medical school, or if they request more elaborate arrangements than those normally provided, the extra expense must be met by the family. Some medical schools give no option on the method or procedure of funerals they arrange.

Chapter 5

After registration

In order to make certain necessary arrangements regarding the deceased's legal and financial affairs, one or more death certificates will almost certainly be needed. These are not the same as the medical certificate of the cause of death signed by a doctor at the time of death, but are certified copies of the entry in the Register of Deaths (the 'standard' death certificate). One certificate each will be needed to apply for probate or letters of administration (see **Chapter 20**), for dealing with the deceased's bank account, and for claims on insurance policies. Each will cost £3.50 (1999/2000, although the cost is likely to increase annually on 1 April) if obtained at the time of registration or within a few weeks afterwards.

If advice is needed about the number and type of certificates required, a list of the purposes for which evidence of death may be required should be taken to the registrar, who will advise accordingly. New death certificates are printed on heavily watermarked paper, and photocopying these is a breach of copyright unless permission to do so is gained from the registrar issuing the certificate, who will advise accordingly.

Notifying the Benefits Agency

The Benefits Agency must be informed about the death in order to deal with pensions and so on; the registrar will provide a free form (**BD8**) for this purpose – this form should also be used to claim various Social Security benefits after someone has died, but it cannot be used to apply to the Social Fund for help with the cost of the funeral. For this, a different form (**SF200**) is needed, which can be obtained from the local Benefits Agency office. The funeral director who is dealing with the funeral arrangements may also keep copies, and will assist

37

with completing them and submitting them to one of the Benefits Agency offices which now deal with them (a pre-paid envelope is normally supplied with the form, or the form may be taken to any Benefits Agency office).

There is no longer any form of general death grant; this was abolished some years ago.

Registrar's certificate for burial or cremation

Together with copies of the death certificate and Social Security Form, the registrar will provide a green certificate (the disposal certificate) to say that the death has been registered and that a funeral may take place. Before issuing this certificate, the registrar must have a properly completed medical certificate of the cause of death signed by a doctor. The registrar's green certificate permits burial or cremation to take place and must be given to the funeral director: the funeral cannot take place without it. If the coroner is involved, a different legal process is involved (see **Chapter 6**).

If the informant is unable to attend the registrar's office within the five days required for notification (see page 15), the registrar, provided he or she has received a medical certificate of cause of death from the doctor, may issue a certificate for burial, but *not* for cremation.

Careful examination of the registrar's green certificate will show whether it has been issued before or after the informant has registered the death: if it states that it was issued *before* registration, it is suitable for burial only, but if issued *after* registration it is suitable for burial or cremation.

The funeral director will send this registrar's certificate either to the cemetery authority or vicar of the churchyard where burial is to take place, or to the office of the local crematorium in the case of cremation.

Obtaining death certificates at a later date

Further copies of death certificates may be obtained from the registrar who registered the death while the current volume of the death register remains in use. This is likely to be about one month, but the time varies according to how many deaths are registered each week and whether the death in question was entered near the beginning or end of the relevant register.

When completed, each death register is passed to the Superintendent Registrar of the district, from whom copies of the death certificate can be obtained later if required. The charge for each certificate in this case is £6.50 (1999/2000).

Applications for certificates by post can be made to the General Register Office.* The charge for this service is £11, but this is reduced to £8 if the index number on a previously issued certificate is known and quoted. If all details of a previously issued certificate have been lost and the office where registration took place is not known, applications should be made to the Public Search Room* in London.

With any postal application, a stamped, self-addressed envelope should be sent, together with a cheque or postal order for the necessary amount. When applying in person to the registrar for a copy of the certificate, payment must be made at the time of application.

Northern Ireland

In Northern Ireland, contact the Registrar General (Northern Ireland).* The charge for a standard death certificate is £7, and the certificate will be supplied within three working days. The charge for additional certificates is £4. There is an express service where certificates may be supplied within one hour; the charge for this is £10, and the charge for certificates at a later date £7. Those wishing to pay by credit card should telephone the special credit-card line.

Scotland

For details regarding registration and obtaining certificates in Scotland, please see **Chapter 7**.

Chapter 6

The coroner

The office of the coroner is ancient: it originated in Saxon times and received a new emphasis under the Norman regime, when the king wanted money to pursue his holy wars. The full title was *Coronæ Curia Regis* (Keeper of the Royal Pleas) and the coroner was responsible for investigating accidents such as shipwrecks – mainly to see what money could be gained for the Crown thereby – and the evaluation of treasure trove. He became responsible for keeping a record of all sudden, unexpected deaths – currently, the subject of most of the coroner's work.

The modern coroner is a qualified doctor or solicitor who is paid by the local authority, but remains independent of both local and central government, being responsible only to the Crown. He or she is assisted by the coroner's officer, usually a police officer; it is the coroner's officer who is generally in contact with the public.

Deaths to be reported to the coroner

When a death occurs which may not be due to natural causes, it must be reported to the coroner. Even if it is fairly evident that death was due to natural causes, but the deceased had not been seen by a doctor for 14 days prior to death, or had not been seen at all by a doctor before or after death, the coroner must be informed. The coroner will then consult with the deceased's GP, who will usually be able to advise whether he or she is satisfied as to the cause of death; the coroner will then cease to be involved and will issue the certificate; the family will then register the death as normal. The doctor is not legally allowed to sign the death certificate if he or she has not seen the patient within this period, even if he or she is confident about the cause of death: the coroner must be consulted. In Northern Ireland, the relevant period is 28 days.

In any case where the doctor is at all uncertain as to the cause of death, the death must be reported to the coroner. Any death attributable to industrial disease, or where compensation has been claimed because of this, must be reported to the coroner (see page 44); in some cases, death caused or accelerated by injury received during military service, however long ago, must also be reported.

Other circumstances in which a death must be reported to the coroner include those when death:

- was sudden and unexplained
- occurred in suspicious circumstances
- was caused directly or indirectly by any kind of accident
- might have been due to neglect, any kind of poisoning, dependence on or abuse of drugs, or abortion
- was by suicide
- occurred while in prison or in police custody
- took place during a surgical operation or before recovery from the effects of anaesthesia.

Reporting the death

Anyone who is uneasy about the apparent cause of a death has the right to inform the coroner for the district. By telephoning a police station, you can find out who the relevant coroner is and how to get in touch with him or her. Or you can give information to any local police station, which will pass the information to the coroner's officer.

The information does not have to be an allegation of some crime. There may be some circumstances which you feel are contributory to the death but may not have been known to the doctor – such as an old war wound or injury – which can be established by a post mortem examination. If you believe that the deceased may have died from some industrial disease, it is obviously best to inform the coroner before the person is cremated, otherwise the matter can never be resolved.

Generally, however, it is the doctor who reports a death to the coroner, or the police. Medical certificates of the cause of death carry a list of the type of cases that the doctor should report to the coroner. If the death comes within any of these categories, the usual practice is for the doctor to inform the coroner directly, before anyone has gone to register the death.

It may be that the registrar, when he or she gets the doctor's medical certificate of the cause of death, decides that because of the cause or circumstances of the death, he or she must report the death to the coroner. In such cases, there will be a delay before the death can be registered, which may interfere with the arrangements that the family had hoped to make for the funeral.

The coroner may decide that there is no need for further investigation, being satisfied that the cause of death is known to be natural, and that the death can be registered from the certificate provided by the doctor. In this case, the coroner sends a formal notice of the decision to the registrar of the district, and the death can then be registered in the usual way by the qualified informant. The chart on page 49 summarises all stages of the process.

If the registrar knows who the next of kin are, he or she gets in touch with them and tells them that he or she is now in a position to register the death. If the death had been reported to the coroner direct and the registrar does not know who the next of kin are, they will have to find out from the coroner's office when to go to the registrar.

Coroner's investigations

When a death is reported to the coroner and he or she decides to investigate, that death cannot be registered until the coroner provides a certificate when inquiries are complete. He or she will usually order a post mortem, which will often show that death was due to natural causes; in this case, he or she will notify the family and the registrar through the coroner's officer, and the death can then be registered in the normal way. If the funeral is to involve burial, the registrar will issue a certificate for burial. If it is to involve cremation, it is the coroner who will issue a coroner's **Form E** for cremation; one part (pink) will be given to the family or sent direct to the registrar, while the other part (yellow) will be sent to the funeral director, or direct to the crematorium.

The actual funeral will have to wait for the outcome of the coroner's investigations, but in many cases the coroner's officer will be able to give a reasonably accurate indication of how long these will take. The funeral director involved will normally consult with the coroner's officer, and will be able to make tentative funeral arrangements while the investigation is proceeding: it is not necessary to wait until the investigation ends before beginning to make arrangements.

In many cases, the coroner's involvement is a formality, and reporting a death to the coroner does not inevitably mean a post mortem or an inquest. The coroner concerned will decide what action must be taken.

Post mortem

The majority of post mortem examinations are ordered by the coroner to establish the cause of death. This may be to show that the death was a natural one or it may resolve a dispute where the family might believe that the death was caused by an industrial disease (a person may have suffered from an industrial illness in life but die from some other, unrelated, cause). In a few cases, the post mortem provides valuable evidence of the manner of a criminal death.

The coroner orders a post mortem if the law requires this. The family of the deceased do not have to be asked to give their consent, as they would be when a hospital wants to perform a post mortem examination. The coroner arranges and pays for the post mortem.

If members of the family object to a post mortem examination for religious or other reasons, or if they have any reason to believe that the examination is not necessary, they should inform the coroner. If the coroner is still of the opinion that the examination is required, the family can apply to the High Court to reverse the decision of the coroner. This will delay arrangements for the disposal of the body.

If the post mortem reveals that the death was due to natural causes and no other circumstance warrants further investigation, the coroner notifies the registrar and the death can be registered in the usual way. In some districts, the coroner's officer or another police officer calls on the family to tell them; otherwise, the next of kin should enquire at the coroner's office every few days to find out when the coroner's notification is being sent to the registrar. The coroner has no duty to inform the next of kin of the result of the post mortem.

After the post mortem, the body again becomes the responsibility of the family. To avoid unnecessary delays, the family can arrange for a funeral director to collect the necessary forms from the coroner's office as soon as these are available and make arrangements for the funeral at the earliest suitable date.

Inquest

The coroner is obliged to hold an inquest into every violent and un-natural death that is reported, and also following the death of a person in prison.

An inquest is an inquiry to determine who the deceased person was, and how, when and where that person died, and to establish the particulars that are required for the registration of the death.

An inquest is held formally and is open to the public. A person wishing to attend, but who has not been given notice of the inquest, can ask at a local police station or telephone the coroner's office to find out when the inquest is being held. The coroner may have asked for further investigations and tests to be carried out, and the date for the inquest will not be arranged until all these are complete.

Adjournments

Coroners are increasingly prepared to open an inquest and then adjourn it 'to a date to be fixed' or for a specific number of days. While police time is not always instantly available, this enables routine enquiries to be completed without holding up burial or cremation arrangements. If it is clear to the coroner that disposal of the body will not prejudice such enquiries, he or she can take evidence of identification and of the cause of death and may then adjourn the inquest, often for a short period, until enquiries are complete – issuing the necessary order for burial or the cremation certificate before the inquest.

Adjournments also have to be made to allow extra time in more complex matters – to await the result, for example, of an inquiry into an air crash or other disaster. The coroner may provide any properly introduced person with an interim certificate of the fact of death. This will allow insurance or other payments to be claimed and the estate to be administered.

An inquest must be adjourned where a person has been charged with causing the death or with an offence connected with it that will be the subject of a trial before a Crown Court jury. The coroner will then send notification to the registrar for the registration of the death.

At the court

The coroner's court is a court of law with power to summon witnesses and jurors, and with power to deal with any contempt in the face of the court.

The law requires that any person with evidence to give concerning the death should attend an inquest. In practice, the coroner will have read any written statements that have been made, and will know the names of those who have been interviewed by the police and by the coroner's officers. The witnesses the coroner knows will be needed are summoned to the inquest. The summons is often an informal telephone call but there may be a written summons or a subpoena (if the witness is outside the jurisdiction of the coroner). A witness is entitled to travel expenses and to a fixed sum to compensate for loss of earnings.

If any witnesses know that they cannot attend, they should inform the coroner's office at once. When a witness has been formally summoned, there are penalties for failing to attend. Non-attendance causes inconvenience, and expense to the family if the inquest has to be adjourned.

Unlike a trial, there are no 'sides' at an inquest. Anyone who is regarded as having a proper interest may ask witnesses questions at an inquest and may be legally represented. The list of people with a 'proper interest' includes parents, children and spouse of the deceased, insurers and beneficiaries of an insurance policy on the life of the deceased, any person whose conduct is called into question regarding the cause of the death, and, in appropriate cases, a chief officer of police, government inspector or trade union official.

There is a minimum amount of pomp and ceremony at an inquest. The coroner calls witnesses in turn from the main part of the court to come up to the witness box. Each witness swears or affirms to 'speak the truth, the whole truth and nothing but the truth'.

First, the coroner questions the witness; then, with his or her permission, the witness can be examined by anyone present who has a proper interest in the case (or by that person's legal representative). If you know that you will want to give evidence or examine a witness, tell the coroner's officer beforehand, so that the coroner can call you at the right moment. When all the witnesses have been heard, the coroner sums up (there are no speeches by the lawyers) and gives the verdict.

With a jury
Some inquests have to be heard before a jury. The jury is summoned in the same way as a crown court jury. In cases of industrial accidents or other incidents that must be reported to a government department,

after a death in prison or in police custody or caused by the act of a police officer, and where death was in circumstances that present a danger to the public, there is always a jury.

The jury for an inquest consists of not fewer than seven and not more than 11 men or women eligible for jury service. There is no power to challenge jurors, as there is no accused person to exercise the power. The jurors are on oath. Jurors need not view the body unless the coroner directs them to.

At the conclusion of his or her enquiries, the coroner sums up the evidence to the jury and explains the law. All the findings of the inquest are then made by the jury. Jurors do not usually leave the court to discuss their decision, but they may do so. They can return a majority verdict.

The verdict

The purpose of an inquest is not only to find out who the deceased person was and how, when and where he or she came by his or her death, but also to decide the category of death. This is colloquially called the verdict but the correct description is the conclusion. It can range from natural causes to suicide, industrial disease or misadventure. Conclusions are subject to many legal technicalities. In particular, the finding of suicide must be strictly proved: when there is no conclusive evidence of the intent to commit suicide, the coroner has to return an open verdict.

The conclusion must not appear to determine any matter of criminal liability against a named person, or any matter of civil liability.

A verdict of accidental death does not mean that there will be no prosecution in a magistrates' court or that the family cannot bring an action for damages. All it means is that it is not a case of suicide or homicide. The 'properly interested persons' are entitled to a copy of the notes of the evidence and these are often useful in subsequent proceedings.

The press and inquests

Since inquests are held in public, the press can be present. There are restrictions on the publication of the names of minors, but in other matters there are no reporting restrictions.

Death is always a sensational subject. Although the coroner may try to choose words carefully, people giving evidence or questioning witnesses may provide comments that can be distressing to the family. The coroner will try to ensure that the facts are as accurate as possible; the inquest may be able to dispel rumours and inaccurate assertions.

The cost

There should be no expense to the family arising out of an inquest. Representation by a lawyer is not necessary in the majority of inquests, and in cases where there is no controversy the family should not need to incur such expense. There is no provision for representation at an inquest under the legal aid scheme.

Many people think it wise, however, to be represented by a solicitor at the inquest in the case of death resulting from an accident or an occupational disease, because there may be compensation claims to be made later and a solicitor would be better able to make use of the evidence presented at an inquest.

Through your local Law Society★ you should be able to find a solicitor who will agree to a free or small-fee interview so that a family does not pay out money unnecessarily. The solicitor may also be able to advise on the possibility of compensation.

After the inquest

In all cases other than those where someone has been charged with a serious offence, the coroner would already have sent the certificate after adjournment, but registration of the death usually takes place when the coroner sends a certificate after inquest to the registrar of births and deaths of the district in which the death took place or in which the body was found. This certificate provides the registrar with the information needed to register the death (see chart opposite). No informant is required to attend the registrar's office. The death certificates can be obtained by the family from the registrar at any time after the inquest.

INQUEST★ provides information and support to people facing the inquest system after a controversial death. They produce a useful pack entitled *Inquests – A Guide for Families and Friends*.

Certificate for burial or cremation

Once a death has been registered, the registrar issues a green certificate, referred to generally as the disposal certificate, authorising either

Procedure following a death

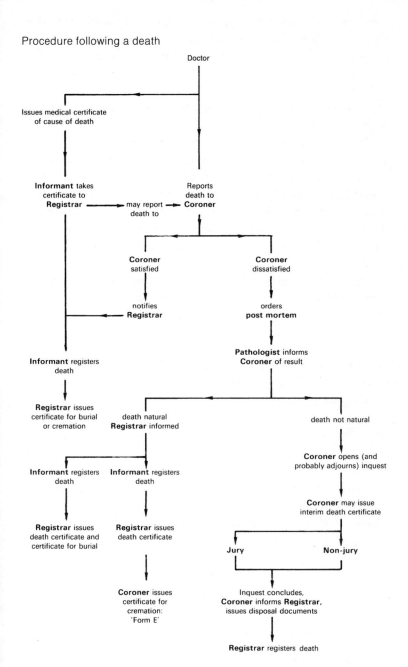

Doctor

Issues medical certificate of cause of death

Informant takes certificate to **Registrar** → may report death to → Reports death to **Coroner**

Coroner satisfied

Coroner dissatisfied

notifies **Registrar**

orders **post mortem**

Pathologist informs **Coroner** of result

Informant registers death

Registrar issues certificate for burial or cremation

death natural **Registrar** informed

death not natural

Informant registers death

Informant registers death

Coroner opens (and probably adjourns) inquest

Registrar issues death certificate and certificate for burial

Registrar issues death certificate

Coroner may issue interim death certificate

Coroner issues certificate for cremation: 'Form E'

Jury

Non-jury

Inquest concludes, **Coroner** informs **Registrar**, issues disposal documents

Registrar registers death

49

burial or application for cremation. A body may not be buried or cremated without this certificate or its equivalent – namely, the coroner's order for burial or certificate for cremation. It is unwise to make more than provisional arrangements for the funeral until you have the certificate from the registrar or the coroner. You will get a burial or cremation certificate from the registrar or from the coroner but not from both.

The registrar can issue a certificate before registering a death but only when he or she has already received the requisite information (including medical evidence) and is just waiting for the informant to come to register the death. This may arise, for instance, when the only suitable informant is ill in hospital but the funeral has to take place. A certificate issued by the registrar before registration authorises burial only; crematorium authorities are not allowed to accept such a certificate.

If the death has been reported to the coroner and a post mortem examination has been ordered, only the coroner can authorise cremation; if the body is to be buried, the registrar can issue the burial certificate. If there has been an inquest, it is the coroner who issues either an order for burial or a certificate for cremation.

No fee is charged for a registrar's certificate or coroner's order. If you lose it, you (or the funeral director) have to apply for a duplicate to the registrar or the coroner who issued the original certificate.

Once you have obtained the necessary certificate from the registrar or the coroner, give it to the funeral director who will take it to the church, cemetery or crematorium officials. Without it, they will not bury or cremate a body. It is the responsibility of the church, cemetery or crematorium to complete **Part C** of the certificate and to return it to the registrar confirming disposal has taken place. If the registrar does not receive Part C within 14 days of the issue of the certificate, he or she will get in touch with the person to whom the certificate had been given to find out what is happening.

Chapter 7

Registration in Scotland

The medical certificate of the cause of death given by doctors in Scotland is similar to that in England. The obligation to give the certificate rests on the doctor who attended the deceased during the last illness but, if there was no doctor in attendance, the certificate may be issued by any doctor who is able to do so. The doctor hands the certificate to a relative to take to the local registrar or sends it direct to the registrar. In the majority of cases, the certificate is issued to a relative.

If a medical certificate of cause of death cannot be given, the registrar can, nevertheless, register the death but must report the facts of the case to the procurator fiscal.

The procurator fiscal

There are no coroners in Scotland and the duties which in England would be carried out by a coroner are in Scotland carried out by a procurator fiscal. The procurator fiscal is a full-time law officer, who comes under the authority of the Lord Advocate.

The procurator fiscal has many functions, including responsibility for investigating all sudden, unexpected and violent deaths and also any death which occurred under suspicious circumstances. If satisfied with the doctor's medical certificate and any evidence received from the police, he or she need take no further action. If, however, the procurator fiscal considers a further medical report is necessary, a medical practitioner (frequently a police surgeon) will be requested to report 'on soul and conscience' what he or she considers was the cause of death.

Post mortem
The procurator fiscal will decide whether or not a post mortem is necessary. In the majority of cases, a post mortem is not carried out and

the doctor certifies the cause of death after an external examination. The mere fact that the cause of death is in a medical sense unexplained is not a ground for ordering a dissection at public expense, provided the intrinsic circumstances explain sufficiently the cause of death in a popular sense and do not raise a suspicion of criminality or negligence.

If a post mortem is carried out, one doctor is usually sufficient but if, while conducting the dissection, the doctor finds unexpected difficulties, the procurator fiscal may decide to bring in a second doctor. Where there is a possibility of criminal proceedings being taken against someone and it is necessary to prove the fact and cause of death, or where the death is drugs-related, a post mortem should be carried out by two medical practitioners.

Public inquiry

Death while in legal custody or as the result of an accident during work must be the subject of a public inquiry (called a Fatal Accident Inquiry or FAI), which takes the place of an inquest in England. If a person, while engaged in industrial employment or occupation, died of natural causes, there may, but will not necessarily, be a public inquiry.

The procurator fiscal has to report certain cases to the Crown Office and it is the Lord Advocate who makes the final decision about whether to apply to a sheriff for an inquiry to be held. In all other cases, investigations made into sudden deaths are carried out by the procurator fiscal confidentially.

Before reporting a case to the Crown Office, the procurator fiscal may interview witnesses and the relatives in private (this is called a pre-cognition).

Cases which are reported to the Crown Office because they may result in a public inquiry are essentially those involving a matter of the public interest – for instance, to prevent a recurrence of similar circumstances. Deaths which are directly or indirectly connected with the action of a third party, such as road traffic deaths, may be reported to the Crown Office for consideration either of criminal proceedings or of a public inquiry.

A public inquiry is heard before the sheriff in the local sheriff court. The procurator fiscal and the representatives of any other interested parties examine the witnesses but it is the sheriff who determines the circumstances of the death.

When the inquiry is completed, the procurator fiscal notifies the result of the findings to the Registrar General. If the death has already been registered, the Registrar General lets the local registrar know if any changes need to be made to the entry. If the death has not already been registered, the Registrar General instructs the registrar of the district in which the death occurred to register the death.

Registering the death

In Scotland the law requires that every death must be registered within eight days from the date of death.

The person qualified to act as informant for registering a death is any relative of the deceased, any person present at the death, the deceased's executor or other legal representative, the occupier of the premises where the death took place, or any person having knowledge of the particulars to be registered.

Whereas in England a death must be registered in the registration office for the district in which the death occurred, in Scotland the death may be registered either in the office for the district in which the death occurred or in the office for the district in which the deceased had normally resided before the death, provided this was also in Scotland. The death of a visitor to Scotland must be registered where the death took place.

As in England, the procedure for registering a death is a simple question-and-answer interview between registrar and informant. The registrar will request the production of a medical certificate of cause of death or, failing that, the name and address of a doctor who can be asked to give the certificate. The information required by a Scottish registrar to register a death is much the same as in England and Wales, except that he or she also needs to know the time of death; if the deceased had ever been married, the name, surname and occupation of each spouse and date of birth of the surviving spouse; the name and occupation of the deceased's father and the name, occupation and maiden surname of the mother, and whether the parents are alive or dead.

When the form of particulars has been completed, the registrar asks the informant to read it over carefully to ensure that all the particulars are correct, and, if a manual registration system is in use, to sign it. (Most registrar's systems are now computerised and it is not necessary to sign. The details of the death will be entered on the computer and the informant will be able to verify these details.) The registrar then makes the entry in the register and asks the informant to check it carefully. The registrar will then also sign the entry.

Registering a stillbirth

A stillbirth in Scotland must be registered within 21 days. As in England, if no doctor or midwife can issue a certificate of stillbirth, an informant must make a declaration on a special form. In Scotland this is **Form 7**, obtainable from the registrar. All such cases, and any case where there is doubt as to whether the child was alive or not, are reported to the procurator fiscal, who notifies the Registrar General of the results of his or her investigations.

If the body is to be cremated, a certificate of stillbirth must be given by the doctor who was in attendance at the confinement (or who conducted a post mortem). The stillbirth must have been registered before cremation can take place.

A stillbirth can be registered either in the district in which it took place or in the district in Scotland in which the mother of the stillborn child was ordinarily resident at the time of the stillbirth.

The informant must produce for the registrar a doctor's or midwife's certificate, or the completed Form 7, and is required to give the same information as in England and, in addition, the time of the stillbirth and, where applicable, the place of the parents' marriage.

Certificate of registration

There is no direct equivalent in Scotland of a disposal certificate (see page 38). After registration, the registrar issues to the informant a certificate of registration of death (**Form 14**), which should be given to the funeral director to give to the keeper of the burial ground or to the crematorium authorities. There is no charge for this certificate.

Death certificates

As in England, the registrar issues, free of charge, a registration or notification of death form which can be used for National Insurance and DSS purposes. All other death certificates must be paid for.

Death certificates are always obtainable from the registrar of the district where the death was registered; they are also obtainable from the General Register Office (Scotland)★ at any time after about a year to

18 months from the date of registration. This is useful if the registration district is not known.

A death certificate (a full copy of an entry in the death register, sometimes called an extract) costs £8 if applied for within one calendar year of the date of registration. It is usual to order death certificates when registering the death. If a certificate is applied for from the registrar or the General Register Office (Scotland) at a later date, the charge is £11 for a personal application or £13 for a postal application. Each certificate beyond the first of the same entry ordered at the same time costs £8 (personal or postal application).

Chapter 8

Decisions about the funeral

When someone dies, a number of decisions about the funeral have to be made quickly. This is often a time of considerable emotional turmoil, so great care needs to be taken to make the right decisions. Many people want to 'get the funeral over with as soon as possible'; it is wise, however, to allow enough time to recover from the shock of the first 48 hours, and plan a funeral which will be an appropriate memorial to the person who has died.

If the deceased left no specific instructions, the decision about burial or cremation is normally made by the next of kin, or the executor. Although it is usual to carry out the wishes previously expressed by the deceased, there is no legal obligation to do so. Should it prove impossible to trace either a living relative or a friend willing to act as executor, the hospital or the local authority will accept the responsibility of providing a minimum-price funeral.

Whether the funeral is to involve burial or cremation, many of the arrangements can be made by a reasonably capable individual who knows what to do. However, most people feel the need of professional help at this time, and it is still rare for a funeral to be carried out without the services of a funeral director.

Funeral directors

William Russell, the first undertaker in the UK, began business in London in 1680; he was succeeded by carpenters who specialised in producing coffins and carriage proprietors who developed special funeral carriages. These functions merged, and a profession of men who 'undertook' to provide a funeral service arose. The Victorian era saw the popularisation of elaborate, often ostentatious, and usually expensive funerals.

Undertakers are now known as funeral directors. The vast majority of funeral directors belong to one of three associations: the Funeral Standards Council (FSC),★ the National Association of Funeral Directors (NAFD),★ or the Society of Allied and Independent Funeral Directors (SAIF).★ SAIF and the FSC broke away from existing trade organisation in 1989 and 1993 respectively; the FSC has recently emerged as the most representative association, comprising the various Co-operative funeral societies, SCI (see page 8), and other smaller groups and independents.

You should be sure to choose a funeral director who is affiliated to one of the three organisations listed above – if the firm is unregistered you might have no form of redress in the event of any problems. The FSC and NAFD have Codes of Practice which include providing information about services and prices, a written estimate of charges and a detailed funeral account. Members must offer a basic funeral if requested to do so. The code covers general and professional conduct, including confidentiality and a procedure for complaints. SAIF has a similar Code of Practice and complaints procedure. Under the code, drawn up in consultation with the Office of Fair Trading, SAIF members are required to refrain from offensive or aggressive marketing techniques; this also applies to the selling of pre-paid funeral plans. The Funeral Ombudsman Scheme★ investigates and resolves disputes between members of the public and funeral directors affiliated to the FSC and the Funeral Planning Council (FPC).★ Although set up by the FSC, it is an independent organisation. SAIF became part of the Funeral Ombudsman Scheme (but not the FSC) in spring 1998. Recent co-operation between the NAFD, the FSC and SAIF has made possible a welcome move towards discussing pre-paid funeral plans with the government.

The funeral director's purpose is to assume total responsibility for organising and supplying all that is needed for a funeral, and to provide as much care as possible for the grieving relatives. A small but increasing number of funeral directors are now offering bereavement care services, with qualified counsellors on the staff. Nevertheless, the arrangement of a funeral is a business transaction and should be treated as such; it is often difficult for bereaved relatives to be businesslike in the circumstances, but most funeral directors are understanding and will give all the assistance needed.

The family should agree who is to be in charge and supervise the arrangements; it is not part of an executor's formal duty to arrange the funeral, although it is a responsibility often taken on.

The cost of the funeral

At the time of arranging the funeral, you should have a fairly clear idea of the kind of funeral that is wanted, and approximately how much money should be spent on it. The funeral director can provide quotations for anything from a basic funeral to an elaborate arrangement costing a great deal of money.

Some people, during their lifetime, take out insurance to pay for their funeral, or join one of the friendly societies which pay out a lump sum on death. Pre-paid funeral plans are becoming increasingly popular: individuals choose the kind of funeral they would prefer and pay for it in advance at a current or slightly reduced rate (see also **Chapter 22**). The scheme concerned should be checked carefully to ensure that the proceeds are safely invested in a trust fund with a nationally recognised trustee, such as one of the high street banks. The scheme should also be affiliated to the National Association for Pre-paid Funeral Plans (NAPFP)★ or the Funeral Planning Council (FPC),★ which co-operate with the Office of Fair Trading to establish guidelines for the protection of clients. At the time of death, all funeral expenses, however they may have increased, are paid for through the scheme. Some schemes, however, reserve the right to make extra charges if the cost of disbursements (such as crematorium or burial fees) rise higher than the rate of inflation. Age Concern★ has now produced its own funeral plan, affiliated to the NAPFP.

Reputable schemes provide peace of mind for many, but the small print always needs to be examined. Some people find the expenses of a funeral very difficult to meet and are embarrassed about telling the funeral director. In fact, one of the first things a funeral director will do is find out whether there is a problem about money and, if there is, whether he or she can help by advising application for a grant from the Social Fund of the Benefits Agency. Normally, the cost of the funeral is paid for from the deceased's estate – the money and property left.

If you require only the most basic kind of funeral, tell the funeral director at the outset; he or she will then tell you what can be provided and how much it will cost. Funeral directors are in business and will bring to your notice all the various services on offer, including providing flowers for the funeral and placing obituary notices in the local and national press. Do not feel pressurised into buying something you do not want.

You can make preliminary arrangements with a funeral director on the telephone, but to make full arrangements for the funeral it will be necessary either for him or her to come to your home, or for you to visit the office. There are papers to be signed and, in the case of cremation, legal documents. The funeral director should show you the price list for the funerals he or she can provide. You can ask for this in advance, and discuss the alternatives with the family. Be sure that you compare like with like: ask for printed price lists, not just a verbal estimate (all funeral directors who are members of the FSC or NAFD must supply these). Ask what is included in any inclusive prices, and visit the funeral director's premises if at all possible. The funeral account will consist of two parts: first, the fees that the funeral director will pay out on your behalf – doctors' fees for cremation papers, crematorium fees, fees for the minister and organist, burial fees, gravedigger, obituary, flowers, etc.; and second, the fees for professional services rendered – removal of the body, preparation and arrangements, use of the chapel of rest, coffin, hearse and limousine, funeral director and bearers etc. He or she will arrange, if asked, for orders of service to be printed and for catering; for most of the disbursements the funeral director will pay in advance, and add the relevant amounts to the funeral account.

The lowest price for a basic funeral starts at not much less than £700. This will vary according to which part of the UK you live in, and will not include disbursements – about £250–350 for cremation, and often a great deal more for burial. For a basic funeral the funeral director will supply a hearse (but not usually a limousine for mourners), a simple coffin and funeral gown, use of the chapel of rest, and the services of a funeral director and four bearers for the funeral cortege, and will conduct all the necessary arrangements and preparation of the body. Many funeral directors will go well beyond the minimum requirements in supplying a basic funeral.

Funeral directors will often quote you an inclusive fee for their services according to the funeral you choose; if special services are required, such as several limousines or a casket for subsequent burial of cremated remains, these will incur extra charges. Many funeral directors make no charge at all for funerals of babies and small children, only passing on disbursements or fees that may or may not be charged by churches or crematoria.

Burial or cremation

The choice of cremation may involve many different factors, but as far as cost is concerned, cremation is usually cheaper. Charges vary around the UK, but an average cost of about £200 for cremation must be set against an average cost of £350–450 for burial in a city's municipal cemetery, although fees in many country cemeteries are often considerably cheaper for residents (fees for non-residents are often doubled and sometimes tripled or quadrupled). Burial in a Church of England churchyard is considerably cheaper – about £185 (plus the cost of digging the grave, about £120–140) – but most churchyards have little grave space left, and can accommodate only the burial of ashes caskets in small plots, or arrange for a second interment in a double grave. In the central areas of large cities, burial fees may increase to many hundreds – sometimes thousands – of pounds.

Many cemetery authorities do not provide the services of a gravedigger; in such cases, allow for the gravedigger's fee (£120–140) as part of the necessary disbursements.

The fees for the services of Church of England churches and clergy are fixed annually by the Church Commissioners, and are followed by most other denominations. The fixed annual fees should include the services of a verger, but extra costs for heating, use of the organ, etc. will often be added; these fees will be the same for burial as for cremation (but see **Chapter 9**, 'Burial').

Coffins

Some funeral directors charge for a complete service, including a coffin, while others break their costs down into charges for vehicles, professional services and so on, and charge separately for the client's choice of coffin. In the case of an inclusive service the choice of a more expensive type of coffin usually provides a more elaborate type of funeral. Different firms include different items in their inclusive charges; some charge extra for mourners' limousines, a car for the minister and for viewing the deceased during evenings or at weekends, while others would include these and other items within the basic fee. A funeral director should be able to show clients examples or illustrations of the different coffins and caskets he or she can supply.

The material from which a coffin is made greatly affects the price: the most basic type of coffin will be made from chipboard laminated with plastic foil; a standard type from wood-veneered chipboard or MDF (medium-density fibreboard); and a superior coffin or casket from solid wood – such as mahogany or oak. A casket is a more expensive form of coffin, which is rectangular instead of the traditional tapered shape. Coffins made of strong cardboard are also now available, but have their limitations as far as strength and attractiveness are concerned. It is advisable to inspect these, as all coffins, before deciding on a purchase.

There is little variation in the cost of coffin linings and fittings, although if solid brass handles are requested, these will be expensive. Remember to notify the funeral director if the coffin should or should not bear a (Christian) cross. For cremation, metal fittings are inadmissible; handles and fittings are made of plastic which has been electroplated with brass or nickel. Indeed, there are rigid by-laws which control the materials used in the construction of coffins for cremation; for each cremation, the funeral director must sign that he or she has conformed to the government's and crematorium's requirements.

Some funeral directors buy plain coffins, which are then lined and fitted with handles according to their client's choice; others offer their clients a variety of coffins already fitted and lined.

Each coffin must be fitted with a nameplate which contains the name of the deceased; it is normal for the plate also to contain the date of death and the deceased's age. It is worth remembering that the coffins offered for simple, basic funerals are intended for cremation rather than burial. In order to keep costs and prices down, the coffin is constructed to be suitable for carrying into a crematorium and placing on the catafalque but may well not be sturdy enough to withstand the rigours of being lowered into a grave. It is advisable to choose a more sturdily constructed coffin if burial is envisaged; this does *not* mean buying the most expensive coffin – the funeral director will advise accordingly.

Other costs

It must be remembered that the total cost of the funeral will consist of the fees the funeral director will charge for his or her professional services, the fees paid to other agencies on behalf of the client, and any special services that are required beyond those supplied in the standard funeral package (such as the removal of a body from a house or nursing home out of standard working hours, additional limousines, and a charge for mileage if the funeral involves travelling some considerable distance). There will also be an extra charge if the body is to be taken into church on the evening before the funeral, or for supplying a casket for the burial of cremated remains (ashes).

The funeral director should give an itemised written estimate of the costs and a formal confirmation of funeral arrangements. Some people may feel that they do not want to be involved in too many practical decisions about the funeral, and want to leave it to the funeral director; it is still important for them to be given a written estimate of the cost. The estimate may well be amended as the bereaved relatives discuss the developing funeral arrangements, and decide on changes, such as the placement of obituaries, or an extra limousine, or indeed reduce the bill by removing various items from the funeral arrangement. The estimate is a clear outline of what the funeral is likely to cost, but is *not* the bill: the funeral director will submit the account shortly after the funeral takes place.

Funeral directors will explain the charges and conditions made for different churches in the local area, and the different fees charged by cemeteries and crematoria. Fees charged for burial in local municipal cemeteries may vary enormously within a short geographical distance, but it is common for local authorities to charge double or treble fees for burials of those who lived outside the local district. Fees for Church of England churches are fixed annually by the church authorities, and normally increase each year. In 2000 the fees for a funeral service in a Church of England church were £66 for the service, and £119 for burial in the churchyard after such a service. Fees for burial in a municipal city cemetery are likely to be much more than this, while fees charged by the cemetery authorities of small towns or villages may well be less. Local churches often charge extra for the services of a verger, for heating, and sometimes for use of the organ (in addition to the organist's fee).

Nonconformist churches usually accept the same fees as those laid down for the Church of England, but frequently waive all charges when the funeral is that of a member of the appropriate congregation. Such churches do not normally have graveyards: church funeral services are usually followed by burial in a municipal cemetery or cremation at the nearest crematorium.

Generally, the total cost of a funeral, including cremation, is unlikely to come to less than £1,000 (2000); burial will probably cost considerably more. If you do not want to pay extra, make sure the price you are quoted is for the most basic funeral available. Price levels, especially for burial, vary enormously between different parts of the UK, especially in London and other large cities; prices also vary between local funeral directors. If you are checking on the cost of funeral services offered in a given locality, it is better to visit the offices rather than telephone; the services offered for a price quoted may vary considerably, as may the quality and condition of vehicles, coffins and so on. No funeral director should object to showing you what he or she can provide, and all members of the FSC or NAFD must be able to give you a price list to take away.

Help with funeral costs

Anyone on a low income who has great difficulty in meeting funeral costs may be able to obtain help from the Social Fund of the Benefits Agency, but there are rigid criteria for gaining such assistance. The applicant or their partner must be receiving one or more of the following: Income Support, Income-based Jobseeker's Allowance, Housing Benefit, Council Tax Benefit, Working Families' Tax Credit or Disability Working Allowance.

This applies *only* to the person arranging the funeral: it makes no difference whether the person who died was receiving one or more of these benefits. In addition, the person applying for the assistance must be paying for the funeral because it was his or her partner who died, or (in the case of the deceased not having a partner), because the applicant for help was what may be described as the next of kin. In this case, the parents (if surviving) and all adult children of the deceased, or their partners, must be in receipt of a qualifying benefit as described above, and be below the savings threshold. Should one of these live overseas, he or she is not likely to be in receipt of UK benefits, and the claim would not be allowed. If the applicant has savings of more than £500 (or £1,000 if over 60), these will be taken into consideration. Awards will not be made if there is a close relative who would be able to pay for the cost of the funeral.

Payments are made from the Social Fund to eligible applicants, and have to be paid back out of the deceased's estate if money becomes available. Funeral directors will usually be able to help eligible clients with an application; the relevant Benefits Agency form is **SF200**, and this, with the account from the funeral director, must be submitted to one of the Benefits Agency offices which currently deal with postal applications.

The Social Fund payment will make provision for up to £600 towards the funeral director's fees, which must include provision of a simple coffin, also the church, minister's and organist's fees. The funeral director's fees will probably amount to more than this; the Benefits Agency maintains that its grant is only *towards* the cost of the funeral. In addition to the £600, payment will be made for the cremation fee at a local crematorium (including the medical referee's fee), the cost of doctors' **Forms B** and **C** (£82 in 1999/2000), and a fee of £63 for the removal of a pacemaker, if fitted. If the funeral involves burial rather than cremation, the grant will cover fees for the purchase of a new grave with exclusive right of burial, interment fees or fees for the re-opening of an existing grave, and the gravedigger's fees. Where neighbouring cemeteries exist with different fees, the cheaper option only will be allowed. The reasonable cost of a journey *either* to arrange *or* attend the funeral will also be allowed, but not both. Allowances for floral tributes or special religious requirements (such as taking the coffin into church the day before the funeral) will no longer be made, unless there is money available from the basic £600 after the funeral director's fees have been met.

If the funeral director's expenses amount to more than £600, or the application for a Social Fund grant is not successful, the person arranging the funeral is responsible for paying the necessary amounts. As changes to the conditions for grants from the Social Fund may occur at short notice, potential applicants should always enquire at the local Benefits Agency, or ask a funeral director. For further information, read the helpful Social Security booklet **D49**, *What to do after a death in England and Wales*, or *What to do after a death in Scotland*. However, do ensure that the details contained in such booklets have not been changed since publication.

A number of local authorities now provide a municipal funeral service. This is done by contracting with local funeral directors for the provision of simple, low-cost funerals for residents of the local authority area. The London boroughs of Lambeth and Lewisham operate such a scheme, and a similar one exists in Cardiff. The cost is considerably less than that of an average local funeral.

Relatives of a member of the armed forces who dies in service may receive help with funeral costs from the Ministry of Defence (see **Chapter 17**).

When someone without relatives dies, and no one can be found to pay for the funeral, the local district council where the person died (or hospital, if the death occurred in hospital) is responsible for arranging the funeral and paying for the cost. If the police have a body in their charge for which no relative can be traced, they notify the local authority which will then provide a minimum-price funeral. Many hospitals have a 'funeral fund' and most local authorities have contracts with local funeral directors for the provision of such funerals. Arrangements vary considerably in different areas. If the provision of such a funeral is likely to be needed, acquaintances of the deceased must not approach any funeral director to begin making funeral arrangements. If they do, responsibility for funeral costs will then fall upon them, as local authorities have no power to reimburse costs where a third party has already made funeral arrangements. The local authority may recoup the cost of the funeral from the estate of the deceased, or from anyone who was responsible for maintaining the deceased while still alive.

Most funeral directors are sympathetic to clients with little money who have to arrange a funeral but do not meet the criteria for a grant from the Social Fund. The majority will provide a basic funeral at minimum cost; it is sometimes possible to spread this cost over a number of monthly payments. The funeral director should be told at the outset if there are financial difficulties, and ways will usually be found to give practical assistance.

Chapter 9

Burial

When someone dies, arrangements for the funeral can be made very quickly, but the date and time should not be confirmed until the death has been registered, and the registrar's certificate for burial (or the coroner's order for burial, should the coroner be involved) has been issued. This must be given to the funeral director; without it, the funeral cannot proceed.

Burial in churchyards

Anyone, whether Christian or not, whose permanent address is within the ecclesiastical parish, is in theory entitled to be buried in the parish churchyard, even if he or she dies away from the parish. In practice, there may be no space left in the churchyard. Many old churchyards are closed to further burials, but some churches have burial grounds separated from the church, where parishioners have the right of burial. Ex-parishioners and non-parishioners with family graves or whose close relatives have been buried in the churchyard have the right of burial there, as does anyone who dies within the parish.

It is the incumbent (vicar, rector or priest in charge) and the parochial church council (PCC) who decide whether someone who has no right by law or custom to burial in the churchyard may be buried there, and what fee to charge. For a non-parishioner, or someone with no connection with the parish, the charges are likely to be higher than for a parishioner.

Burial fees

For people who live within the boundaries of the local parish, certain fees are payable to the local church for funeral services in church followed by burial in the churchyard. A proportion of these fees is paid to the incumbent as a contribution towards his or her salary, and the remainder to the PCC; these fees are specified by the Church Commissioners under the Parochial Fees Order, and usually increase annually.

The current fee payable for a funeral service in church is £66, and the fee for a subsequent burial in the churchyard is £119: a total of £185 (2000). If the church service is followed by burial in a municipal or private cemetery, the church fee of £66 remains the same, but the interment fee is paid to the local authority or owners of the cemetery and will vary considerably; no interment fee is payable to the church. Any payment for an organist, choir or bell ringers is additional; there is often a charge for heating and the use of the organ, in addition to the organist's fee. The services of the verger should be included in the fee of £66, to be paid out of the proportion allowable to the PCC.

The fee for burial in a churchyard without having had a service in a church of the parish beforehand is £143; the same fee is payable if the churchyard burial does not take place immediately following the church service, but takes place on a subsequent occasion. If a graveside service is held before a churchyard burial, the fee of £66 remains, plus the interment fee of £119; the cost is the same as if the service had been held in the church. No fee is payable for the burial of a stillborn child, or for the funeral or burial of an infant who died within one year of birth.

If, after cremation, the cremated remains or ashes are to be buried in the churchyard, the fee will be £60; there is no longer a different fee for burying ashes loose or in a casket. If the crematorium service has been a simple committal and the funeral service is to be held in the churchyard when the ashes are buried, a further fee of £66 is incurred – the same as for a service held in church. This fee does not apply, however, if the incumbent attends the burial of the ashes and provides a simple service of committal, but a fee of £24 is often charged – the portion of the fee for burial of ashes in a churchyard that is paid directly to the incumbent.

Gravediggers' fees are in addition to the above. If the parish has its own gravedigger, the fee is likely to be between £60 and £120; if the funeral director provides the gravedigger, the fee is likely to be between £90 and £140. These fees will vary according to place and circumstances, and are likely to rise annually – sometimes considerably.

The grave

Paying a burial fee does not buy the right to choose the location of the grave in the churchyard. The vicar allots the site. Nor does the burial fee entitle you to ownership of the grave or to the exclusive right of burial in that grave.

By faculty

If you want the exclusive use of a plot in a churchyard, you must apply to the diocesan registrar to reserve a grave space, by a licence called a faculty. Although a faculty gives the right to say who can be buried in the plot, the freehold of the ground continues to belong to the Church.

The fee charged by the diocese for a faculty depends on the amount of work involved in the petition. It takes about six weeks for a faculty to be granted. When a person dies, it is too late to get a faculty for him or her, but the relatives could apply for a faculty to reserve the grave for other members of the family. Anyone arranging a burial in a grave reserved by a faculty must produce the faculty or other evidence which proves his or her right to the grave.

The incumbent charges a fee for the first and each subsequent interment in a grave reserved by faculty. An additional charge is made for removing and replacing an existing headstone to enable subsequent interments in a grave to take place.

Burial inside a church

Today, any rights an incumbent may have had in the past to consent to a burial inside the church building have become obsolete. Faculties to permit such burials are rarely granted and in urban areas burial in and under a church is prohibited by law.

Burial in cemeteries

Most cemeteries are non-denominational, and are run either by a local authority or by a privately owned company. A few cemeteries are owned by a particular denomination; burial in such places is usually restricted to members of that denomination.

Some cemeteries have a section of the ground consecrated by the Church of England, while the opening of many new cemeteries (the old ones are filling up) is attended by a service of consecration for the whole of the area.

The fee payable to a member of the Church of England clergy for conducting a service in a cemetery or crematorium is the same as that for a funeral service in church: £66 (2000). There is no church fee, however, if the burial immediately follows a church service. Should the cemetery burial take place some time after a funeral service in church, a fee of £24 is payable in addition to the £66 fee for the church funeral service.

Some cemeteries have ground dedicated to, or reserved for, other specific religious groups, and a separate section of general ground. In most cemeteries, any type of religious service (or none at all) can be held. Most cemeteries have a chapel which is non-denominational, and can be used for funeral services when a service in the church is not desired. However, it should be noted that many of these are seldom used: a considerable number have neither lighting nor heating and may be damp and somewhat dilapidated.

Some cemeteries provide the services of a chaplain for burial services on a rota basis; where this is in effect, there is usually a choice of Roman Catholic, Church of England or Free Church.

Fees

Fees for burial in a cemetery vary widely even within the same locality. They are set by the owners, under the terms of the appropriate Acts of Parliament. Fees and regulations are usually displayed at the cemetery. If you write to the superintendents of the local cemeteries, you will be sent lists or brochures, from which you can compare the charges and conditions. A cemetery's fee may include the services of a clergyman and gravedigger; some will not allow flowers to be planted or put on graves; others will not permit any memorial to be put up, except over the more expensive graves or for a limited number of years only, after which the cemetery authorities can remove it. Conditions or payments for maintenance are often stipulated.

In most local authority cemeteries, a higher fee is required for those who are not residents within the local council district; these are usually double the normal fees, but may be treble, or even more. There may be some concessions for former residents and their relatives. Interment fees are less for children than for adults; each cemetery authority fixes its own fees and defines its own age limits.

Cemetery burial fees are usually in two parts: there is a charge for purchasing the exclusive right of burial in a certain plot and an additional charge for interment. These charges vary enormously, especially in inner cities. The purchase of an exclusive right of burial used to be known as 'buying a plot'; most authorities will sell a lease on a plot for a certain period of time, so that only the purchaser or his or her family may be buried there. The terms of the lease were traditionally 99 years, but 75 years is now common, and some exclusive rights of burial are available for only 50, or even 25 years.

Most local authority cemeteries have an application form which the executor or next of kin is required to sign. All fees have to be paid in advance, and all the required documents sent to the cemetery office by a stipulated date before the funeral. This will normally be dealt with by the funeral director; the client will then have the fees added to the funeral account and repay the funeral director on presentation of the account after the funeral.

Graves

In most cemeteries, there are various categories of grave.

The cheapest are graves without the right to exclusive burial. The person paying the interment fee has no right to say who else may or may not be buried in the grave. The graves are marked by a number; it may be possible to put up a small memorial or plaque, although frequently this is not allowed. In some cemeteries, no interments will take place in such a grave for a set number of years – usually 7 or 14 – after the last burial, except to bury another member of the same family.

In a few cemeteries, for a small fee a grave space can be reserved for a specified period of years from the date of payment. After this, it reverts to the cemetery unless a further fee has been paid either to reserve the space for a further period or for the exclusive right to the grave on behalf of the person buried in it; thus it becomes similar to a private (or purchased) grave.

In most cemeteries, you can buy the right of exclusive burial in a particular plot, in a similar way as by a faculty granted for a grave in a churchyard. The right used to be in perpetuity, but nowadays it is more usually granted for a specific number of years – for instance, 50.

For a private grave, you get a deed of grant (sometimes referred to as a certificate of ownership), for which some cemeteries make a small

Documents for burial

Document	Source	Function	Recipient
registrar's certificate for burial (the disposal certificate) or if inquest is to be held: coroner's order for burial	registrar coroner	required before burial can take place authorises burial	via relative and funeral director to burial authorities; Part C returned to registrar
application for burial in cemetery	from cemetery via funeral director, usually signed by executor or next of kin	applies for burial and confirms arrangements	cemetery authorities
grave deeds or faculty	cemetery or diocese	proves right to grave	burial authorities
copy of entry in burial register	burial authorities	proves burial and locates grave	executor or next of kin

charge. The deed should be kept somewhere safe and the family or executors should know where it is. It may have to be produced in evidence before the grave can be opened for an interment. Usually the signature of the owner of the grave is required on the cemetery's application form to authorise the opening of a private grave. If the owner of the exclusive right of burial has died, the cemetery will probably require some alternative formality to authorise the use of the grave if the right had not been re-registered following the death of the owner. Afterwards, the deed will be endorsed with details of the burial and returned to the executors. An interment fee has to be paid in addition, and also a fee for removing and replacing an existing headstone.

Another category of grave is the 'lawn grave', in which you have the right to exclusive burial, but can put up only a very simple headstone, leaving the rest of the grave as grass. Kerbs, surrounds and elaborate memorials are not permitted. This type of grave is easier to maintain, and consequently most modern cemeteries permit lawn graves only. Enquiries must be made as soon as possible if anything other than a simple headstone is envisaged, as considerable distress can be caused if an elaborate memorial is planned and restrictions are discovered only after the burial has taken place.

On cemetery plans, various categories of grave are shown; where this is applicable, fees will depend on the type, size and depth of the grave. In older cemeteries, normal unlined graves are referred to as 'earth graves'; 'brick graves' have a bricked (or concrete) floor and walls and are much more expensive. Where these are still available, longer notice of burial and higher interment fees are often required.

Formalities and the construction of a brick grave can take weeks; these are now very unusual.

Burial at sea

Burial at sea is both complicated and expensive, but it is possible at certain places along the coast of the UK (see **Chapter 17**).

Other burial grounds

If you want to be buried in ground other than a churchyard or cemetery, the law stipulates that such private burials must be registered. Even if you are the freeholder of the land, you must ascertain from the deeds whether the land is restricted in the use to which it may be put. If you want to bury someone in your garden, you are advised to consult your local planning authority and environmental health department.

Woodland burial

A number of woodland, or 'green' burial grounds have made their services available recently; these concentrate on keeping the environment as natural as possible, and plots are available in meadowland or woodland. Normally no memorial stone or tablet is permitted, and the wild nature of the environment is encouraged. The charges imposed by these woodland burial grounds may not be significantly lower than those levied by municipal cemeteries, and in some cases are higher than those at normal country cemeteries nearby.

Chapter 10

Burial in Scotland

The certificate of registration of death which the registrar has given to the informant must be given to the person in charge of the place of interment or cremation. No part of the certificate is returned to the registrar.

Burial

In Scotland a grave is referred to as a lair. As in England, it is possible to purchase the exclusive right of burial in a cemetery or kirkyard plot, either in perpetuity or for a limited period. Cemeteries are administered by the local council. In Scotland, cemetery chapels are rare.

At burials in urban cemeteries, silk tasselled cords, called courtesy cords, are attached to the coffin. Specific mourners are sent a card beforehand inviting them to hold a cord while the coffin bearers take the strain of the lowering. In most country areas the cords actually take the weight. Courtesy cords are not used for the burial of cremated remains.

A pad or mattress is often put on top of the coffin as a development of the old custom of putting grass or straw over the coffin to muffle the sound of earth falling on the lid when the grave is filled in.

In Scotland by tradition women did not go to the interment in the graveyard after the church service. This practice has been abandoned by and large, although it still survives occasionally, especially in the older generation.

Cremation

The regulations and procedure for cremation are the same as in England and Wales since the Cremation Regulations 1965 brought these into line with those of Scotland.

Sending a body abroad

There are no formalities connected with the removal of bodies out of Scotland for either cremation or burial in another country, but you should ensure that the death has been registered in Scotland before moving the body out of Scotland. The procurator fiscal does not have to be informed.

If the body is being taken to England or Wales for burial, the certificate of registration (**Form 14**) or the standard death certificate must be produced for the registrar there.

No formal notice has to be given or permission sought when cremated remains are being taken out of the country.

Bringing a body from abroad

There is no need to produce evidence for the registrar in Scotland that the death took place elsewhere. If the body is coming from England or Wales, the person in charge of the place of interment or cremation in Scotland will require the coroner's form permitting the body to be removed.

When a body is brought into Scotland to be cremated there, the authority of the Secretary of State for Scotland must be obtained before cremation can be carried out. This means applying to the Scottish Office Department of Health,* with any supporting papers, such as a foreign death certificate.

Cremated remains brought into Scotland must be accompanied by a certificate of cremation issued by the crematorium.

Chapter 11

Cremation

In most areas, the majority of funerals involve cremation rather than burial. This is due not only to the fact that cremation is cheaper, but also to a radical shift in attitudes that has developed since cremation began to be popular in the early years of this century. Before cremation can take place, the cause of death has to be ascertained beyond any reasonable doubt. If the deceased's doctor knows the cause of death, he or she will sign the medical certificate of the cause of death, and an additional certificate of examination which must be corroborated by another doctor. If he or she does not know the cause of death, the coroner must be informed and, ultimately, will issue a coroner's certificate for cremation. Unlike burial, which can sometimes take place on the authority of a disposal certificate issued before registration, cremation cannot take place until the correct certificates have been produced and the death registered.

The formalities

Four statutory forms have to be completed before cremation can take place; one by the next of kin or the executor, the others by three different doctors. The forms are issued by the crematorium; funeral directors keep a supply and doctors usually keep a supply of those relevant to them.

Form A is the application for cremation, and has to be completed by the next of kin or the executor, and countersigned by a householder who knows him or her personally. In most situations, the funeral director will be acceptable as counter-signatory, but some crematoria insist on someone else signing the form.

Forms B and **C** are on the same piece of paper, which also often includes **Form F**. **Form B** has to be completed by the doctor who attended the deceased during the last illness; he or she must examine the body before the form can be completed. This may or may not be the patient's normal GP. The doctor may have to ask the relatives or acquaintances for some of the information the forms require: for instance, whether the deceased has undergone any operation during the final illness, or within a year before death, whether the deceased had been fitted with a pacemaker, and whether or not it had been removed (pacemakers must be removed before cremation to avoid an explosion).

Form C is the confirmatory medical certificate, and must be completed by a doctor who has been registered as a medical practitioner in the UK for five years or more. He or she must not be a relative of the deceased, nor a relative or partner of the doctor who completed **Form B**. If two hospital doctors complete **Forms B** and **C**, they must not have worked on the same ward, attending the same patient. The second doctor also has to see the body before completing the form.

Form F, the fourth statutory document, has to be signed by the medical referee of the crematorium, stating that he or she is satisfied with the details on **Forms B** and **C**, or the coroner's certificate for cremation. The medical referee has the authority to prevent cremation taking place and may query details given in the forms supplied. If it is felt necessary, he or she may order a post mortem to take place, or refer the matter to the coroner, if this has not already been done. The relatives of the deceased have no right to prevent this post mortem; if they do not wish it to take place, then they must forgo cremation and opt for burial instead. If they do agree to the post mortem, it is quite likely that they will have to pay for it. This is extremely unusual, however: the funeral director and crematoria staff will usually notice any anomalies before it reaches the stage of submission to the medical referee. Most crematoria include the fee for the services of the medical referee in the total charge for cremation.

When the coroner is involved and has ordered a post mortem, he or she will issue a certificate for cremation for which there is no charge; in this case, **Forms B** and **C** are not required. When a death is reported to the coroner, he or she must be informed at the outset if the funeral is to involve cremation, so that the appropriate certificate may be issued. This is statutory **Form E**, and (if there is to be no inquest) will be supplied as a pink form to the relatives so that they may register, and as a yellow form to the funeral director for submission to the crematorium. Sometimes the appropriate forms may be sent by the coroner direct to the registrar and crematorium.

In very rare cases where the coroner has a reason for not allowing cremation to take place, he or she will issue a coroner's order for burial only. The coroner may be able to inform the relatives that cremation may be possible at a later date, when the investigations have been completed; the relatives in this case must be prepared to wait for cremation at a later date, or opt for burial.

If the body of a stillborn child is to be cremated, a special medical certificate has to be completed by a doctor who was present at the birth, or who examined the body after birth. No second medical certificate is required, but the medical referee still has to complete **Form F** (see below). Many crematoria charge no fees for the cremation of stillborn children, or infants up to the age of one year.

The table on page 82 summarises the function of each form.

Fees

Fees for a cremation funeral include the charges made by the crematorium (which usually include the fee for the medical referee, who has to sign **Form F** before the cremation can take place), the fees for the doctors' certificates and, normally, a standard fee for the minister who takes the service. Sometimes the organist's fee is included in a charge levied by the crematorium, although at other times he or she is engaged separately and charges a separate fee. All these are normally paid in advance by the funeral director, and added to the final funeral account.

The fees charged by crematoria vary from one district to another, but are generally in the region of £125 to £250, with additional fees normally charged for those who did not live in the local district. Unlike burial fees, these are not usually doubled, but involve only a relatively small extra charge.

The doctors who prepare and sign **Forms B** and **C** are each entitled to a fee; the British Medical Association fixes a minimum fee which changes annually on 1 April. The fee for each part was £41 in 1999/2000. A fee of £63 may also be charged by a doctor for removing a pacemaker, which is essential if cremation is to take place; this removal, however, may be carried out by the funeral director's staff as part of his or her inclusive charges. Doctors are also entitled to charge travelling expenses of 56.4p per mile (1999/2000) when signing forms for cremation, but in practice may not do so for short distances of a few miles.

Sometimes, when death has occurred in hospital, the hospital may wish to carry out a post mortem examination to improve understanding of the patient's medical condition. This is not mandatory, and the consent of the relatives must be obtained; if given, **Form C** will not be required, providing that the post mortem is carried out by a pathologist of not less than five years' standing and the result known by the doctor who signed **Form B**. Hence only one fee of £41 will be charged, unless the pathologist was of less than five years' standing; in this case he or she may still carry out the post mortem, but another doctor who does have five years' standing must complete **Form C** and the full £82 will be charged.

Most crematoria charge reduced fees for the funerals of children up to school-leaving age; practices vary, but the fees are often in the region of 20 per cent of the full adult fees. As already stated, there are usually no fees for stillbirths or infants up to about one year old.

Crematoria

The majority of crematoria are run by local authorities, although some are privately run. Each crematorium has its own scale of fees: considerable variation exists. Many have brochures giving details of what they offer, and the fees charged: most organise annual 'open days', usually on a Sunday, when the general public can investigate the whole cremation procedure. Most crematoria are open Monday to Friday only; a few are open on Saturday mornings, and some will offer cremation outside normal working hours at an extra charge, which is usually quite considerable.

The government has recently brought in new regulations regarding pollution and the environment; for many crematoria this has meant that new cremators have had to be installed in order to conform with the regulations. This has been enormously expensive, and many crematoria have raised their charges in order to assist with the cost.

The service

Charges for cremation usually include a fee for the use of the crematorium chapel, whether or not it is used for a religious service. The chapel is non-denominational, catering for a range of religions. Some crematoria have a rota of chaplains of various denominations, but usually arrangements for a clergyman to conduct the funeral service are made by the relatives or the funeral director. There is no law requiring a religious service at a funeral, and a small but growing number of people opt for a non-religious funeral service. The British Humanist Association★ or the National Secular Society★ will put you in touch with someone in your area who can conduct such services; most funeral directors will be able to refer you to someone, and some are experienced themselves at conducting such services.

Most crematoria have facilities for playing music while the congregation enters and leaves, and this may be chosen by the relatives.

Crematoria work to a strict appointments system, so services must be fairly short, unless a special booking is made for a longer period, which will cost extra. Most crematoria allow 30 minutes between appointments, some allow 45 minutes, and some only 20 minutes.

Memorials

Most crematoria have various forms of memorial. There is usually a 'Book of Remembrance' in which the name of the deceased may be suitably inscribed; other memorials involve small stone wall-plaques, memorial rose bushes with a plaque giving the name of the deceased, or a display of spring flowers. Few now provide a columbarium, where ashes may be stored in a small niche in a special wall, but some crematoria allow ashes caskets to be buried in that part of the grounds known as the 'Garden of Remembrance', or in an adjoining cemetery.

All of these will involve special charges, and are usually offered to the bereaved a couple of weeks after the funeral. Do not allow yourself to be pressurised into buying a memorial that is not something you really want. Take time to consider all the options and costs, and discuss the matter thoroughly with all involved. You may decide that you do not want any form of memorial.

Some new or recently refurbished crematoria provide extensive means of memorial in carefully landscaped grounds. Some have made

Documents for cremation

Document	Source	Function	Recipient
registrar's certificate for burial or cremation (green certificate) *or*	registrar	required before funeral can take place	via relative and funeral director to crematorium authorities; Part C returns to registrar
coroner's certificate for cremation: Form E	coroner after post mortem or inquest	replaces Form B/C	
Form A	funeral director or crematorium: to be completed by executor or next of kin	applies for cremation and confirms arrangements	crematorium
Form B*	doctor or hospital	certifies cause of death	medical referee at crematorium
Form C*†	doctor or hospital, to be completed by second doctor	confirms cause of death	medical referee at crematorium
ashes disposal form	funeral director or crematorium	confirms arrangements, gives instructions for disposal of ashes	crematorium authorities
Form F	medical referee	confirms information in Forms B & C or E	crematorium authorities
certificate for disposal of cremated remains	crematorium	confirms date and place of cremation	via relatives to burial authorities
certificate of cremation	crematorium	copy of entry in register	executor or next of kin

*Forms B and C are not required if the coroner is involved and issues Form E
†Form C is not required if a hospital post mortem is conducted by a doctor qualified for more than five years

new provision for the storage or burial of ashes caskets, and one or two have created elaborate water gardens with provision for personal memorials to be set in place.

Cremated remains

The cremated remains or ashes of the deceased may be scattered in the grounds of the crematorium, taken away to be scattered elsewhere, or buried in a local churchyard or cemetery. The crematorium will not normally charge a fee for scattering ashes shortly after the funeral, but a fee will be incurred if the ashes are stored and scattered at a later date. There will also be a fee – about £25 – if the ashes are to be scattered in the grounds of a different crematorium from the one where the funeral took place.

The Church of England charge for burial of ashes in a churchyard is £60 (2000). Fees for the interment of ashes in municipal or private cemeteries vary enormously.

Some crematoria are reluctant to arrange the transport of ashes from one locality to another. The funeral director will be able to arrange this, or a local courier or parcels service will do it within the UK for a fee of around £15 upwards.

During 1999, considerable publicity was given to the matter of the dignified disposal of human organs removed for medical research during post mortem examinations, especially in relation to babies and small children. Relatives faced distress as it was not at this time legal to cremate these organs separately, some time after the funeral had taken place. In February 2000 the law was changed to allow crematoria to participate in such disposals. Those concerned should consult their local crematorium superintendent, who will be able to advise accordingly.

A leaflet, *Questions People Ask*, answering queries about cremation, is produced by the Federation of British Cremation Authorities, and is available from some crematoria.

Chapter 12

Before the funeral

Most funeral directors maintain a 24-hour service; if a death occurs at home or in a nursing home out of office hours, two members of the funeral director's staff who are on duty at that time will come very quickly to take the body to the mortuary. Nursing and retirement homes normally want the body moved as soon as possible. It is rare, nowadays, for a body to remain at home for the interval between death and the funeral, although it is possible if the relatives request it. Unless the relatives intend arranging the funeral themselves, the funeral director should be approached as soon as possible after the death occurs. In many cases, the member of staff with whom you have the first interview will remain in charge until after the funeral is completed.

The body

About 80 per cent of people currently die in hospital, and half of the remainder in nursing or retirement homes. Of the remaining 10 per cent who die at home, the great majority are taken to the funeral director's premises to await the funeral in a chapel of rest; this is a small room where the deceased remains in a coffin until shortly before the funeral. Laying out, or 'first offices' (known as 'last offices' in hospital), almost always takes place at the funeral director's mortuary. If the deceased is not to wear his or her own clothes, the funeral director will supply a funeral gown as part of the inclusive service. He or she will want to know what the family would like to do about any jewellery worn.

When someone dies in hospital, the body is normally taken to the hospital mortuary; however, a number of (usually small) hospitals now sub-contract mortuary facilities to a local funeral director. When a death occurs, the funeral director's staff will remove the body to his or her mortuary, where it will remain until cremation papers (if needed) have been completed. If the coroner is involved and decides that a post mortem is necessary, the funeral director's staff will take the body to the coroner's mortuary. The relatives are not obliged to make use of the services of this funeral director; he or she will co-operate with the funeral director chosen by the relatives.

If the body is taken to a mortuary on the hospital premises outside normal working hours, the hospital will not normally permit it to be moved until the next day. If the coroner is involved, the body cannot be moved until he or she is satisfied that the necessary papers can be issued.

When the funeral director's staff come to remove a body from a house or hospital, they normally use a large estate car adapted for the purpose. Sometimes an ambulance is used; very rarely, a hearse. The staff will normally use a covered stretcher; sometimes, a form of coffin designed for removals called a 'shell'. The funeral director usually needs written authority in order to remove a body from hospital; this normally takes the form of the green certificate issued by the registrar (registrar's certificate for burial or cremation), which means that registration must be attended to as soon as possible. An authorisation signed by the next of kin or executor is sometimes acceptable.

When the body is kept in a chapel of rest, relatives and friends can go to see it before the funeral; the funeral director will usually ask for an appointment to be made so that a member of staff can be available to give the family undivided attention. Sometimes extra charges are made for viewing the body at evenings or weekends. Relatives often like to leave some personal memento in the coffin, but are embarrassed to ask; funeral directors will often suggest that photographs, letters, flowers etc. may be placed in the coffin with the deceased. Where cremation is involved, it is important that these mementoes are combustible.

Some larger firms of funeral directors also have their own chapel for private prayer, in which a religious service can be held at the beginning of the funeral before the cortege leaves for the cemetery or crematorium.

Embalming

Embalming is a process intended to delay temporarily the process of decomposition, and involves replacing the blood in the arterial system with a preservative, normally a solution of formalin. The process is similar to a blood transfusion, and is sometimes called 'preservative' or 'hygienic' treatment. It bears no resemblance to the ancient Egyptian process of mummification.

Embalming is advisable if the body is to be returned to a private house to await the funeral, or if the funeral is to be held more than four or five days from the date of death and the body cannot be kept in cold storage. Some bodies begin to decompose much sooner than others; a bad appearance and odours can be extremely distressing for a family who wish to view the body. Some funeral directors embalm every body brought on to their premises, while others do so only if they consider it necessary. Sometimes there is an extra charge for embalming. If relatives of the deceased do not want the body to be embalmed, they should discuss the matter with the funeral director.

Before a body can be embalmed the doctor must have completed the medical certificate of the cause of death, and the death duly registered. Where cremation is involved, **Forms B** and **C** must also have been completed (see pages 77–8). If the coroner is involved, embalming must not take place until his or her authority has been obtained. An embalmer should be qualified by examination, and abide by the code of practice laid down by the British Institute of Embalmers. In the UK, embalmers tend to make minimal use of cosmetics (unless requested to do so by the family); the aim is to present as natural an appearance as possible, as if the deceased were asleep.

In a hospital mortuary, the bodies are kept refrigerated; most funeral directors also have cold-storage facilities, sometimes combined with deep-freeze facilities so that bodies can, if necessary, be kept for some considerable time before the funeral takes place. This may be necessary where a member of the family is abroad and cannot be contacted or where a close relative is in hospital awaiting recovery.

Final arrangements

The funeral director must have the registrar's disposal certificate (or the coroner's equivalent authorisation) before confirming the final arrangements. He or she will see to it that all official forms are completed and taken to the right people at the right time. For a burial, for instance, he or she takes charge of any grave deeds and gets a cemetery's form of application signed by the executor.

In effect, the funeral director should co-ordinate the various operations at the different stages. He or she will approach the people in charge of wherever it has been decided the burial or cremation is to take place (this usually means the local clergyman or superintendent of the cemetery or crematorium) in order to reserve a time and, for a burial, to order the type of grave required.

For a cremation, the funeral director sees that a relative or the executor completes the form of application and the form giving instructions for disposal of the ashes and will also arrange for two doctors to complete **Forms B** and **C**. He or she will pay them their fees and, when the necessary forms have been gathered, will pass them to the medical referee at the crematorium.

Most crematoria produce at least one other form on which the person organising the funeral confirms any details already provisionally arranged, such as the date and time of cremation. Some crematoria ask on this form for specific instructions about the disposal of the ashes; others have yet another form for this.

The forms have to be submitted to the medical referee of the crematorium by a stipulated time – which is never less than 24 hours before the cremation is due. The reservation of a time for the cremation is accepted subject to the forms reaching the crematorium within the specified time limit and the fees being paid in advance.

The fees – to vicar, sexton, gravedigger, organist, choirmaster, chaplain and officials at the cemetery or crematorium, as the case may be – usually have to be paid in advance. The funeral director will make the actual payments and will add the charges to the total account.

The service

Either the funeral director or a member of the family should ask whoever the family wants to officiate at any service, whether he or she is willing to do so and whether he or she will be available at the time planned for holding the ceremony. The minister will probably visit the family, particularly if the deceased had an active church connection, to offer consolation and also to arrange practical details of the service.

There is no obligation to have a service in church; services can be held in the churchyard, cemetery, crematorium chapel, village hall, or any other suitable building. Unlike weddings, funeral services may be held in any building, and no special form of registration or licensing is necessary. A Church of England funeral service can be conducted by the incumbent or, with his or her permission, by any other clergyman, such as a member of the family or the clergyman whose church the deceased normally attended.

If you want a particular piece of music to be played, you should ask for this when making arrangements for the service.

A service in a crematorium or cemetery chapel is restricted by the time allowed – normally half an hour.

Most religious denominations have some form of funeral ceremony. In this country, unless the dead person had professed another religion, one of the Church of England services will probably be said at the funeral.

Rituals can be adapted according to the preferences of those concerned. For instance, the main part of the service can be said in the church or at the funeral director's with only a few words of committal at the graveside, or all the service can be at the grave. A funeral address may be given either in the church or outside, or not at all.

If you are having an unusual form of service, you can arrange through the funeral director or officiant for special service sheets to be printed.

Non-Church of England funerals

Denominational burial grounds usually insist on their own form of service. If you are arranging the funeral of someone of a faith different from your own, get in touch as soon as possible with the equivalent of the local parish priest of that denomination to find out what needs to be done. (See also **Chapter 14**.)

For a practising Roman Catholic, it is usual to arrange for the priest to say a requiem mass in the local parish church and for him to take the funeral service. There are no set fees laid down for Roman Catholic priests to charge for funeral services, but it is usual for the deceased's family to make an offering to the church. Cremation is no longer discouraged for Roman Catholics, and crematoria have Roman Catholic priests on their roster.

With Orthodox Jews, the body should be buried as soon as possible once the disposal certificate is issued. If a man subscribes to a synagogue burial society, he or his wife or his dependent children will be buried, free, by the society in its cemetery. The funeral and coffin will be very simple, and there will be no flowers. Orthodox Jews are never cremated, and embalming or bequeathing a body for medical purposes is not allowed. Reform non-orthodox Jews are more flexible, and permit cremation. The funeral will always be simple, but flowers are allowed. A Jewish burial society may agree to carry out the funeral of a Jew who was not a member of a synagogue and had not been subscribing to any burial society, but his family will be charged for the funeral and the cost will be considerable. There is rarely any difference between the funeral of members of the same synagogue; all are simple. If a Jew dies when away from home, it is the responsibility of the relatives to bring the body back at their own expense for the synagogue burial society to take over.

Non-religious services

There is no necessity to have a religious ceremony, or indeed any kind of ceremony at all, at a funeral. However, because some kind of religious ceremony is customary, if you do not want one or the dead person had made it clear that he or she did not want one, it is important that the executor or whoever is in charge of the arrangements makes this known well before the funeral.

If a body is to be buried in a churchyard without a religious ceremony, or with a ceremony held by an officiant of another denomination, you should give the incumbent of the parish 48 hours' notice in writing; in practice, it should be possible to make the necessary arrangements in a telephone conversation. The usual parish regulations and fees still apply.

If a body is to be buried in a cemetery or cremated at a crematorium without a religious ceremony, tell the funeral director or the authorities at the time the funeral is being arranged. There will normally be no difficulties, provided it is clear that the proceedings will be properly conducted. Where there is not going to be a religious ceremony, whoever is in charge of the funeral arrangements must also make arrangements for the details of the ceremony.

If you want no ceremony at all, the usual procedure is for a few members of the family or close friends to attend the committal in silence or with some music being played. If you want a non-religious ceremony without an officiant, on the lines of a Society of Friends (Quaker) meeting, you must make sure that those present either know already how such a ceremony works or are told at the beginning.

The more usual procedure is to have an officiant who prepares and conducts the ceremony, on the lines of a minister. This may be a member of the family or a close friend, or a representative of an appropriate organisation or a sympathetic religious minister. The only qualification is some experience of handling meetings. Business, professional and labour organisations generally contain such people, as do humanist societies.

The national freethought organisations in London all give help with funerals: they can offer information and advice by telephone or post, send out literature, and sometimes provide officiants for funerals. The British Humanist Association★ has a network of humanist funeral officiators who can be contacted by calling the 24-hour national helpline. Other agencies include the National Secular Society,★ the Rationalist Press Association★ and the South Place Ethical Society.★ The British Humanist Association charges £5 (inclusive of postage and packing) for its booklet *Funerals Without God: A Practical Guide to Non-religious Funerals*, and the other organisations appreciate donations for their material. Officiants would expect to be paid a standard fee plus expenses, normally about the same as the fee set for church ministers.

A non-religious ceremony may take any form, provided it is decent and orderly. The usual procedure is for the officiant to explain the ceremony, after which there may be readings of appropriate prose or poetry, tributes either by the officiant or others present, and the playing of appropriate music. It is common to allow a time of silence when the deceased may be remembered personally, and religious people may offer silent prayers. These ceremonies are not intended to oppose religious funerals, but are alternatives for people who would feel it hypocritical to have a religious service, or who want a respectful celebration of the death that has occurred without a religious emphasis.

Press notices

Announcements of deaths are usually made in local papers, and sometimes the national dailies; the cost for an average obituary in a local paper is likely to be about £40, and in a national paper about £150. Newspapers will not normally accept text for obituaries by telephone, unless placed by a funeral director; even then there is a rigorous call-back and checking system because of many distressing hoaxes. The papers do not usually ask for evidence that the death has occurred, unless the notice is submitted by someone who is not a relative, executor, or funeral director.

National daily newspapers will insist on a standard form of announcement, and will restrict the words that can be used. Most funeral directors are well aware of the system, and will advise accordingly. The address of the deceased should *not* be inserted into the obituary: too many houses have been burgled while the funeral is taking place. Where there is anxiety about this, the funeral director may be able to supply a member of staff as 'house sitter' for the duration of the funeral service.

The majority of funerals currently give people the opportunity of making donations to a nominated charity in memory of the deceased, as well as, or in place of, flowers. It is normal for the funeral director to collect such donations and forward them in due course to the charity concerned, informing the relatives of the amount collected. This information is usually contained in the obituary, and the funeral director's name and address is given so that information can be given and donations made.

Details of the date, time and place of the funeral can be included in the obituary. Anyone who has not been specifically invited but wishes to attend is expected to arrive independently at the time and place announced in the press. If the family want to restrict attendance at the funeral, the obituary should state 'private funeral service', or the equivalent; in this case, only those invited by the family should attend. If the family think that a great many people may wish to attend, arrangements may be made for a funeral service in a large church or auditorium followed by cremation or burial which is attended only by the family and close friends; alternatively, a private funeral for the family only may be followed some time later by a memorial service and all who wish to pay their last respects to the deceased may attend.

If no details of the time or place are published, it should be assumed that the funeral is to be private.

Flowers

The press notice should make clear whether there are to be no flowers, family flowers only, or the option of a memorial donation. A 'no flowers' request should be strictly observed. Flowers are normally sent to the funeral director's premises; most florists are aware of this, and will contact the funeral director to ask what time flowers should be delivered. It is not normal for press notices nowadays to say where flowers should be sent: the funeral director will collect any that are sent to the family home when he or she calls at the house for the funeral service, and will normally supply the family with a list of those who sent flowers when submitting the account. Flower cards may be collected and returned if the funeral director is asked to do so.

When a body is buried, flowers are normally left on the grave after it has been filled in. At the crematorium, there will normally be restrictions as to where flowers can be placed, and the length of time they will be displayed: some are on display for only 24 hours after the funeral, others for a week, and others are regularly cleared once a week. Traditional wreaths are rare nowadays; it is common for the family to request flowers in the form of bouquets or arrangements that can be taken to hospitals or old people's homes after the funeral service has been completed.

Chapter 13

The funeral

Traditionally, the cortege (or funeral procession) started at the house where the deceased lived, with the hearse and one or more cars for the mourners travelling by a pre-arranged route to the church or crematorium. This still frequently happens, but it is as common for the hearse to travel directly to the location of the funeral from the funeral director's premises; the mourners will then be brought to meet it by either their own or the funeral director's vehicles. If the funeral director provides cars for the bereaved relatives, he or she will marshal the cortege and arrange its departure.

Timing is most important, because cemetery and cremation authorities work to a very tight schedule; if the funeral cortege arrives too early or too late, it will probably interfere with the preceding or following funerals. Should it arrive considerably late, especially at the crematorium, it is possible that the funeral service will have to be drastically shortened, or even postponed, to the great distress of the relatives.

The funeral director should have discussed all the details of the funeral with the family beforehand, and arrange where people are to be taken after the funeral, whether the minister requires transport, what happens to the flowers etc.

If you are worried that the house may be burgled while the funeral is taking place, the funeral director may be able to provide a member of staff as a 'house-sitter'. The funeral director should not incur any additional expenses without the client's authority.

It is unlikely nowadays that the funeral director will ask relatives if they would like to witness the closing of the coffin immediately before the funeral, but customs vary in different parts of the UK.

The funeral director may walk in front of the hearse as it leaves the deceased's house, and again as it approaches the church or crematorium; this is not only as a mark of respect, but to enable him or her to direct the traffic and keep the funeral cortege together, especially as it leaves a side street to enter a main road. The coffin will normally be carried into the church or crematorium on the shoulders of four of the funeral director's staff, although in some places a small trolley is used for moving the coffin. Sometimes, members or friends of the family are able to act as bearers; this makes for a closer participation in the funeral, and the funeral director's staff will still be on hand to assist and give directions. Occasionally, at more formal funerals, pall-bearers walk alongside the coffin, apparently fulfilling no purpose. Traditionally, these used to carry the 'pall', a heavy fabric canopy which was held over the coffin. Today, the pall is normally used to cover the coffin in the hearse if it has to travel some considerable distance between towns before the funeral cortege can gather; it is then removed, and the family flowers are placed on the coffin before it moves off.

Burial

Where a burial is preceded by a church service, the coffin is taken into the church by the bearers and placed on trestles or a trolley in front of the altar. In Roman Catholic and some other churches, the coffin may be taken into church before the funeral, often the previous evening, and remain there until the funeral service takes place. Most funeral services in church take about half an hour, although a requiem mass, or the funeral of a well-known member of the church congregation, may take an hour or more. After the service, the bearers will take the coffin from the church, either to the churchyard or, more commonly, to the local cemetery, usually led by the minister and funeral director. If burial is not preceded by a church service, the coffin is carried direct from the hearse to the graveside, where there is normally a short service.

The coffin will be lowered into the grave by the bearers while the words of committal are said; this part of the funeral service is quite brief, and normally lasts about five minutes. In Scotland, the coffin is usually lowered by members of the family. Sometimes the mourners throw a token handful of earth into the grave, or each drops a flower on to the coffin; they do not normally (except in Ireland) remain to see the grave filled in – this is done later by the cemetery staff or grave-digger.

A register of burials in the parish is kept by the church; every cemetery has to keep a register of burials and records of who owns a grave plot, and who has already been buried in each grave. Copies of the entries in these registers can be obtained for a small fee.

When someone is buried in a Church of England churchyard the family is responsible for looking after the grave. The PCC (parochial church council) is responsible for looking after the churchyard generally, and for keeping the paths and unused parts tidy. Some dioceses stipulate that, before a funeral takes place, a contribution must be made towards the upkeep of the churchyard. Municipal and private cemeteries will employ groundsmen to take care of grounds and graves; this upkeep is often difficult and costly, which is why most authorities now stipulate lawn graves only: graves with a simple headstone in line with other headstones, and no kerbs or surrounds to interfere with mechanical mowing. However, where there are gravestones, whether simple or elaborate, the holder of the grave deeds is responsible for their upkeep; this can become very expensive as stones weather and crack, and ground settles over the years. Upkeep of memorial stones is often neglected – another reason why authorities prefer to stipulate lawn graves only.

Many churches place quite rigid restrictions on the type of memorials and stone which may be used in churchyards. It is essential to check with the local church before placing an order with a stonemason; funeral directors will be aware of the requirements of local churches and will be able to advise accordingly.

Cremation

Traditionally, the funeral service prior to cremation was held in church, with the congregation (or only the chief mourners if the cremation was to be private) travelling to the appropriate crematorium for a brief committal afterwards. Increasingly, funeral services are held entirely in crematorium chapels; the hearse and cars go straight to the crematorium and the bearers carry the coffin into the chapel and place it on the catafalque. Usually, the mourners follow the coffin into the crematorium, led by the minister and funeral director but, increasingly, people prefer to enter the chapel and sit down before the coffin is brought in.

When the words of committal are spoken, the coffin passes out of sight; it will either sink into a recess or pass through a door, or a curtain will move in front of it. Some people prefer the coffin to remain on the catafalque until the mourners have left the chapel; this option is available if requested. During the funeral service, the funeral director's staff will take flowers from the hearse and place them in the floral display area; when the coffin moves out of sight at committal, the flowers on the coffin will be retrieved and added to the display. Some crematoria will only keep flowers on display for the day following the funeral; others leave them in place for several days, while yet others clear them once a week. The funeral director will take appropriate sprays and arrangements to hospitals or nursing homes after the mourners have departed if requested to do so: these are often greatly appreciated.

When the coffin moves out of sight, it is taken to the committal room to await cremation. Each coffin is loaded individually into a cremator, once the name on the coffin plate has been checked by the crematorium staff. It is illegal to remove the coffin from the crematorium, or (other than the flowers) anything from the coffin, once the committal has been made. When the cremation process is complete, after two to three hours, the ashes are refined separately and placed in carefully labelled containers; each cremator must be cleared totally before another coffin can be loaded.

When making arrangements for the cremation, the next of kin or executors can ask to be present when the coffin is placed in the cremator; this is especially relevant for Hindu funerals, where traditionally the next of kin would light the funeral pyre. Usually, two people only are allowed.

Each crematorium has to keep a register of cremations. A certified copy of the entry in the register is obtainable for a small fee. It is unlikely that such a certificate would be necessary, unless the death had not been registered in the UK, or the ashes were being sent to another country which required such a certificate.

The ashes
When making arrangements for the funeral, the clients will be asked what they would like done with the ashes. Most are scattered, or

buried loose beneath the turf in the crematorium grounds; they can, however, be taken away by the next of kin or executor for disposal elsewhere, for example, scattering in a place meaningful to the deceased or family, or burial in a churchyard or cemetery. If a family grave already exists, the ashes may be buried in that grave for a fee, usually around £60. If a plot for the burial of ashes has to be purchased (i.e. where no family grave exists), there will (except in churchyards) be a fee for the exclusive right of burial. Cremated remains can usually be obtained from the crematorium on the day following the funeral; however, providing notice is given in advance, ashes may be obtained on the same day if the funeral takes place before midday.

Crematoria are not normally willing to post or otherwise send cremated remains to other locations. However, most funeral directors will take them short distances by car or arrange for national transportation by a courier. It is difficult and expensive to send them by post yourself but if you wish to do so you should consult one of the national parcel services. Costs are usually between £15 and £30 inland, and about double to Ireland or any of the UK coastal islands.

Most crematoria will arrange for a monthly fee to store ashes until they are required; funeral directors will do the same, but most will probably not charge for storage. Funeral directors will also supply caskets for burial of ashes, or simple urns for storage or scattering. These vary in price from about £15 for a simple urn to several hundred pounds for an elaborate casket. Decisions about or arrangements for the eventual disposal of ashes need not be made at the time of the funeral. However, if there is even the remotest likelihood that the crematorium will *not* be required to scatter the ashes in its grounds, this should be made clear at the outset. It is easy to scatter ashes later, but, obviously, impossible to do anything else with them once they have been scattered. Normally, at the time of signing statutory **Form A** (see page 77), the next of kin or executor will be required to fill in a form on the reverse giving instructions for the ashes.

When the ashes are taken away, the crematorium normally provides a free certificate confirming that the cremation has taken place. This document has no legal significance, but is sometimes requested by church or cemetery authorities when the ashes are to be buried.

If ashes are to be scattered in the grounds of a different crematorium, or the same crematorium at a considerably later date, there will be an additional fee of around £10–30. If a funeral director has to arrange for ashes to be buried in a different location or at a considerably later time, he or she will charge a fee in addition to the inclusive fee for the funeral.

There is no law regulating the disposal of cremated remains; ashes can be scattered anywhere, providing the scattering is done respectfully, and with the consent of the owners or executors of private grounds, such as golf courses, etc. The funeral director will arrange to scatter the ashes for clients in a chosen location and will not normally charge for this unless considerable time and travelling expenses are incurred.

The crematorium grounds are usually known as a 'Garden of Remembrance'; such ground is not usually consecrated, and the place is not normally marked. Some crematoria scatter the ashes around on the surface of the grass or earth; others remove a small portion of turf, pour the ashes on the ground and then replace the turf. Some allow a casket containing the ashes to be buried in the grounds. The family can choose a spot and witness the proceedings if they request to do so; some crematoria charge a fee for this. There is generally no formal ceremony for the scattering of ashes; the burial of a casket is, however, frequently attended by a minister who conducts a brief service of committal.

Parish churches of the Church of England will frequently allow only ashes to be buried in churchyards, as there is little room left for full burials; fees for this were £60 in 2000. Most churches will allow the placement of a small stone plaque, inscribed with the name of the deceased, where the ashes are buried. As with headstones, there are usually rigid restrictions about the type and size of stone that is accepted. Each church tends to have its own interpretation of regulations, and it is essential that enquiries are made at the appropriate church as to what memorials are allowed before the interment takes place; church stipulations may not be acceptable to the relatives, in which case interment elsewhere must be considered. A fee will be charged for placing the memorial stone, in either churchyard or cemetery.

A final word: if a decision is taken to scatter the ashes, and this is to be carried out by the family, it is important to ensure that the mourners stand with the wind behind them.

Chapter 14

Non-Christian and minority group funerals

In today's multi-ethnic society, and especially in inner-city areas, many funerals do not conform to the traditional Christian approach that has been the main emphasis of this book so far. This chapter briefly and simply outlines the practices of other faiths of which there are now large numbers of adherents throughout the UK.

Muslims

Muslims live according to a strict moral code which has specific prescriptions concerning death and burial. There are numerous Muslim sects, each with its own variation of funeral rites, but in the UK about 90 per cent are Sunni Muslims, and the remaining 10 per cent are almost entirely Shia Muslims.

Muslim communities normally appoint one person to represent them in making funeral arrangements, who will usually deal with one approved funeral director in the locality. The representative will advise on the rules, which are strict and need to be followed as closely as possible.

Muslims are always buried, never cremated. Traditionally there is no coffin – the body is wrapped in a plain white sheet and buried within 24 hours of death in an unmarked grave, which must be raised between 4 inches and 12 inches from the ground, and must not be walked, sat or stood upon. Most cemeteries in Britain, however, require a coffin for burial or cremation. Many British cemeteries insist on levelling the graves as soon as possible, which has led to some authorities providing special areas for Muslim burials; where there is none, families can suffer great distress. Because of the need for haste in burials, requests for post mortems and organ donation are usually, but not always, refused.

Muslims believe that the soul remains for some time in the body after death, and the body remains conscious of pain. Bodies must therefore be handled with great care and sensitivity, and disposable gloves worn at all times by those handling the body: the body must never be touched directly by a non-Muslim. Embalming is not normally practised, but is permissible where the body has to be conveyed over long distances.

Normally, the family will attend to laying out the body, and they will turn the head over the right shoulder to face Mecca, which is roughly to the south-east. The body will be wrapped in a plain sheet and taken home or to the mosque for ritual washing: men will wash male bodies, and women female. Camphor is normally placed in the armpits and body orifices, and the body will be dressed in clean white cotton clothes or a special white shroud brought back personally from Mecca.

The funeral service will take considerable time. There will be ritual washing, at least 30 minutes of prayer at the mosque, possible return to the family home, prayers at the graveside and the filling in of the grave. Relatives and friends will carry the coffin at shoulder height, passing it from one to another, and they will want to see the face of the deceased after the final prayer at the graveside. Muslims must be buried facing Mecca, with the head over the right shoulder; hence graves must lie north-east/south-west, with the head at the south-west end. The family will normally perform all rites and ceremonies, together with the imam, the spiritual leader of the local mosque.

Hindus

Hindus, unlike Muslims, do not normally insist on one approved funeral director to handle funerals; there is no central authority for those who adhere to this religion, and rites and customs vary enormously.

There are thousands of Hindu deities, which are all held to be manifestations of the same God. The three main deities are Brahma, the Creator; Vishnu, the Preserver; and Shiva, the Destroyer. Hindu belief in reincarnation means that most individuals face death in the hope of achieving a better form in the next round of life. Death is therefore relatively insignificant, although there is likely to be open mourning with much weeping and physical contact by family and friends. There are normally strong objections to post mortem examinations, which are held to be deeply disrespectful to the dead.

Hindus are always cremated, and never buried. Prior to the cremation, most Hindus bring their dead into a chapel of rest, where the body must be wrapped in a plain sheet and placed on the floor. Most light lamps or candles, and those who come to view will probably burn incense sticks. There are normally no objections to the body being handled by non-Hindus, but this and all burial rites are capable of great variation. The family concerned will be explicit about the rites required by their form of Hinduism. The Asian Funeral Service★ arranges Hindu funerals and organises repatriation for those who require a funeral by the Ganges.

Sikhs

Sikhism developed from Hinduism in the fifteenth century and has much in common with it, but with a strong emphasis on militarism. There is a common belief in reincarnation, and the fact of death is normally accepted calmly.

There are five symbols of faith which are vitally important to every Sikh. The *Kesh* is the uncut hair which, for men, is always turbaned. The *Kangha* is a ritual comb to keep the hair in place; this is never removed. The *Kara* is a steel bracelet worn on the right wrist (or left if left-handed); the *Kirpan* is a small symbolic dagger, which may actually vary in size from a brooch to a broadsword – and the Sikh will never be separated from it. Finally, the *Kaccha* are ceremonial undergarments which are never completely removed, even while bathing. Sikhs are always cremated, never buried; the Sikh family will insist in every instance that their dead are cremated with all five 'K symbols' present. Considerable diplomacy may be required to satisfy both family and crematorium authorities.

After death, men are dressed in a white cotton shroud and turban; young women are dressed in red, and older women in white. The family will almost always want to lay out the body, and will want cremation to take place as soon as possible – in India, it would normally be within 24 hours. The coffin will normally be taken home and opened for friends and family to pay their last respects and will then be taken either to the *gurdwara*, for the main funeral service, or direct to the crematorium, where the oldest son will, instead of lighting the traditional funeral pyre, press the crematorium button or see the coffin into the cremator. The ashes will be required for scattering in a river or at sea; it is not unusual for one member of the family to take them to India to scatter them in the Punjab.

Stillborn babies, by exception, are usually buried.

Buddhists

Buddhism is the main religion in many Far-Eastern countries such as Burma and Nepal, but it is still relatively rare in the UK. After death, Buddhists will have the deceased person wrapped in a plain sheet and prepared for cremation. Buddhists of different nationalities have widely varying funeral customs, and nothing can be assumed to be held in common.

Jews

Scattered from their homeland by the Roman army in AD70, the Jews dispersed across the world and adopted many different practices and interpretations of the Mosaic Law, yet always maintaining their essential unity. Orthodox Jews believe that the Law was literally handed to Moses by God, while Progressive Jews (divided into Reform, Liberal and Conservative groups) believe that the Law, while inspired, was written down and influenced by many different authors. Orthodox Jews are therefore extremely strict on the observation of funeral rites, while Progressive Jews vary in their attitudes.

When a Jew dies, the body is traditionally left for eight minutes while a feather is placed on the mouth and nostrils to give any indications or signs of breathing. Eyes and mouth are then closed by the oldest son, or nearest relative. Many Jews follow the custom of appointing 'wachers': people who stay with the body night and day until the funeral, praying and reciting psalms. The dead are buried as soon as possible. No Orthodox Jew will accept cremation, although it is becoming increasingly favourable among some Progressive groups. Orthodox rabbis will sometimes permit the burial of cremated remains in a full-sized coffin, and say *Kaddish* (the mourner's prayer) for the person concerned.

Jewish funerals are usually arranged by a Jewish funeral agency (such as United Synagogues). Otherwise, the local Jewish community will arrange a contract with a Gentile funeral service, under which all Jewish funerals will be carried out according to strict rabbinical control. If a secular Jew is appointed as executor, or is responsible for making funeral arrangements, it is essential that enquiries are made into the religious background of the deceased, so that the appropriate rabbi may be contacted.

Jewish coffins are as simple and plain as possible, usually with rope handles and written nameplates. Embalming does not take place, and mourners do not view the body.

The Jewish Bereavement Counselling Service* offers support to those who have lost loved ones.

Cults

There are now a great variety of Christian cults, or diverging Christian groups, which include the Mormons, Jehovah's Witnesses, Christadelphians, Christian Scientists, Scientologists, the Moonies and the Children of God. For most, while differences in doctrine are held to be immensely important, there is little deviation from orthodox Christian practice as far as funerals are concerned. Funerals may well take longer, which may cause difficulties in fitting in with crematorium schedules.

Some groups, such as Bahai and Hare Krishna, are basically Hindu derivants, and may adhere more closely to Hindu funeral rites than any other.

Much New Age culture is basically a westernised form of Hinduism, and those who practise yoga or transcendental meditation may adopt the Hindu philosophies which lie behind them, which will in due course affect the funeral arrangements that will need to be made.

Chapter 15

Arranging a funeral without a funeral director

When a close relative dies, most people prefer someone outside the immediate family circle to undertake the responsibility of arranging the funeral and attend to all the necessary details. Most want to 'get the funeral over with' as soon as possible, and are reluctant to be involved any more than is necessary in making arrangements for, and participating in, the funeral service. However, human reactions to grief follow a fairly standard pattern (see **Chapter 18**), and it is an established fact that personal involvement in arrangements for the funeral assists the grieving process and hastens a healthy recovery.

Such participation will, for most people, seldom involve more than laying out and dressing the deceased, viewing the body in the chapel of rest, providing family bearers to carry the coffin and participating in the funeral service. It is, however, perfectly possible to arrange the whole funeral yourself; there can be considerable snags and difficulties, but with knowledge and determination, these can be overcome.

Arranging the funeral

Assuming that the coroner is not involved, the doctor's medical certificate of the cause of death must be obtained, and the death registered. The necessary papers must be obtained and submitted to the cemetery or crematorium with the appropriate fees. A date and time for the funeral must be arranged with the same authorities – if a church service is to be held, the church and minister must be consulted before that time is confirmed. If a minister is to conduct the funeral service, he or she must be asked to do so, again before confirming the time. A coffin will normally be required, and a decision made about where the body is to be kept until the funeral. Means of conveying the coffin to the church, cemetery or crematorium must be obtained. If the funeral is to involve burial, a gravedigger must be hired, or the decision taken to dig the grave oneself. If the grave is to be on private land (i.e. not in a churchyard or cemetery), it is wise to inform the local planning authorities. Bearers must be found to carry the coffin.

These constitute the necessary minimum; several of the above involve forms which take time and patience to obtain and process.

Cremation

Cremation is a much more common option than burial – currently, 80 per cent of funerals involve cremation.

You must first obtain two doctors' certificates for cremation to take place (**Forms B** and **C**, both normally on the same piece of paper). If the deceased died in hospital, the hospital must be asked for the papers; if death occurred at home, the doctor who had been attending the deceased must complete **Form B** and another, independent, doctor, complete **Form C**. Each doctor will require the standard fee for completing the forms (£41 in 1999/2000). If the deceased was fitted with a pacemaker, this must be removed, normally by the doctor completing **Form B**; a separate fee of £63 will be charged for this. If the doctor has to travel beyond a minimum distance to complete these papers, he or she is entitled to charge 56.4p per mile, although many do not charge for short distances of a mile or two.

The next of kin or executor will need to obtain statutory **Form A** from the crematorium; this is the application for cremation, and will be accompanied by the crematorium's own administration form. Both must be completed and submitted to the crematorium with the doctor's **Forms B** and **C**, the registrar's green certificate for burial or cremation, and the appropriate fee. Many crematoria also require a signed form giving instructions about the disposal of cremated remains; this is often printed on the reverse of **Form A**, but is not a statutory form and is not itself part of **Form A**. The documents required for cremation are described in **Chapter 11**.

Most crematoria insist that a coffin be used (for the exceptions, consult the Natural Death Centre).★ The crematorium's administration form will include a signed declaration that the coffin conforms to legislation relating to pollution of the environment. This is important: people have in the past constructed coffins for loved ones and brought them to the crematorium only to be refused permission to cremate because the coffins did not conform to the necessary requirements. These requirements are usually printed on the crematorium's application form, and can be obtained from the local crematorium.

Burial

Burial has fewer problems than cremation, provided it is to take place in a churchyard or cemetery. No doctors' certificates (**Forms B** and **C**) are required, but the registrar's green certificate for burial or cremation (see page 38) must be submitted to the church or cemetery authorities, together with, in the case of a municipal or private cemetery, a completed application form and the required fee. A date and time for the funeral must be agreed. A gravedigger must be found and hired: the churchyard may have its own gravedigger.

Coffin

For those with the ability, it is possible to construct a suitable coffin at home. It must be strong enough to cope with the stress imparted by an inert body being carried and lowered by inexpert bearers, and be made of suitable material: some cemeteries will not allow the burial of any metallic coffin or casket. In the case of cremation, the coffin must be made of materials that conform to the specifications laid down by the crematorium; these are usually printed on the application form, and it is normal practice for a signature indicating compliance to be required. A reasonable degree of expertise and experience are required: it is far from funny when a coffin collapses at a funeral, and no one should contemplate beginning a d-i-y career by making a coffin.

Coffins can be purchased from funeral supermarkets, and some funeral directors are willing to supply them. In an attempt to make funerals more environmentally friendly, biodegradable cardboard coffins have recently been introduced. These can be obtained from several sources from about £60 plus delivery: the Natural Death Centre★ will give advice. Prospective purchasers should be warned that cardboard coffins have their limitations regarding both strength and appearance. Wickerwork coffins are now available from several suppliers: these are relatively expensive.

Waiting for the funeral

A decision must be made as to where the coffined body is to be stored until the funeral takes place. This will usually be a room of the house, which will need to be kept as cool as possible. Ensure that all heating is turned off, and that there is constant ventilation. Some diseases cause bodily decomposition to begin far more quickly than normal: it may be necessary to arrange for the body to be embalmed, especially in summer. Portable air-conditioners may be hired from an equipment-hire company to help keep the temperature low.

If the deceased died in hospital, it may be possible for the body to remain in the hospital mortuary until the day before the funeral.

Funeral transport

The coffin can be taken to the funeral in the back of a large estate car, Land Rover or horse and carriage. Hearses and horse-drawn hearses can be hired if preferred. It is unwise for bearers to carry the coffin any further than is strictly necessary.

Burial at home

It is possible to arrange for a burial to take place on your own land – in a garden or field. It is wise to advise local planning authorities of your intent; planning permission is not strictly necessary, but restrictions may be made if the local water table is likely to be affected. If such a private burial is to be considered, it should be discussed with the appropriate authorities long before death is expected to take place.

There are other potential difficulties to be considered. Should relatives of the deceased decide for any reason to move house, the presence of a grave in the garden may present problems. The emotional decision to leave the grave must be faced, as must the fact that its presence will mean that the selling price of the house will almost certainly drop by 25–50 per cent. If the family wants to take the body to a new location, a Home Office licence for exhumation will be required; application must be made on forms which the Home Office will supply. The cost of the licence itself is £10, but the process of exhumation is likely to be expensive and to involve practical and psychological difficulties. The authority concerned will probably insist on experienced grave-diggers being employed for the job, among other requirements. Exhumation without a licence is a criminal offence.

Unless a small part of private grounds can be set aside in perpetuity as a private cemetery, which may well be possible on an estate, farm or family house with a large garden, arrangements for burial at home are likely to present difficulties. A reasonable solution to this problem is to arrange for a cremation, and then to scatter or bury the ashes in the garden or field. Technically, an ashes casket buried in private ground is subject to the same laws of exhumation as a coffin; it can, however, legally be moved from one part of the private grounds to another. If ashes caskets are 'buried' *above* ground in, say, a purpose-built rockery or mausoleum, the casket can be moved elsewhere without difficulty.

Funeral management schemes

Many funeral directors are eager to see their clients more involved in funeral arrangements, being aware that this will assist them in the grieving process. Some offer a service to clients who want to arrange funerals for their relatives themselves, and are prepared to sell them a coffin at a reasonable price, hire out a hearse if so required and provide a management service for a set fee. The service would provide all the necessary documentation, with advice on how and where to make the necessary arrangements.

If, however, a client decides to pay a management fee, buy a coffin, hire a hearse and then pay the funeral director or hospital mortuary staff to prepare the body, rent a chapel of rest etc., the overall cost will probably be more than if a funeral director had been asked to make all the necessary arrangements in the first place.

Helpful advice on organising a funeral yourself can be obtained from the Natural Death Centre.* The centre also publishes the *Natural Death Handbook*, which gives advice and information on all aspects of arranging and conducting funerals yourself. This can be obtained from the Centre at a cost of £11.65 including postage and packing, or £12.14 if paying by credit card.

Funeral supermarkets

A number of 'funeral supermarkets' have opened in Britain. Shoppers take a trolley and can choose everything from a coffin to silk flowers; trained staff are on hand to advise on both what to buy and how to arrange funeral services.

Chapter 16

After the funeral

When the funeral service has finished, family and friends often gather for light refreshments at the house of the deceased, at the house of another member of the family, or at a local public house or restaurant. If required to do so, the funeral director will book catering at a local public venue, or arrange for caterers to come into the house during the funeral and provide for guests. Mourners need to be clearly informed about what has been arranged, and where they are to go.

Paying for the funeral

The funeral director will submit an account fairly soon after the funeral, and will appreciate payment as soon as possible: he or she has already paid out quite substantial sums for various services to enable the funeral to take place – but will, of course, understand if the account cannot be settled until a grant of probate or letters of administration have been issued (you must make this clear). All the major banks will release funds from frozen accounts to enable the funeral bill to be paid, if provided with a suitable funeral account from the funeral director. Legally, payment of the funeral bill is the first claim on the estate of the deceased, taking priority over income tax and any other claims.

The funeral director's account should be as detailed as possible, showing separately what has been paid out to doctors, crematoria, ministers etc. on your behalf, and what is due to his or her company as the fee for professional services rendered. This will enable you to verify that only authorised payments have been made. Any gratuities given to mortuary or cemetery staff by the funeral director are normally considered as part of the inclusive charge; any tips to bearers or others officiating at the funeral would be at the discretion of the client.

All the payments that the funeral director will have made on behalf of the client should be expenses that would inevitably have been incurred; in addition to the necessities, he or she may have been asked to provide flowers, place obituary notices in newspapers, provide catering and service sheets, etc.

The services of the funeral director, minister and cemetery or crematorium are exempt from VAT. VAT must, however, be paid on flowers, catering, printing, and any form of memorial.

Memorials

Relatives often want to place a memorial tablet or headstone in a churchyard or cemetery where a coffin or ashes casket has been buried. Both churchyards and municipal cemeteries impose restrictions on the size and type of memorial and on the kind of stone that may be used and the type of lettering inscribed on it. Many cemeteries and almost all churchyards currently prohibit kerbs or surrounds to graves, and memorials are often restricted to a headstone or a plinth and vase set at the head of the grave.

Neither reserving a grave in a churchyard by faculty (where this is still possible – see page 69) or purchasing the exclusive right of burial in a cemetery provides the right to putting up any kind of memorial. For this, approval must be gained from the respective authority and a fee paid. The Church Commissioners in the Parochial Fees Order lay down the charges for memorials in the churchyards of the Church of England. Fees in 2000 were as follows:

- small wooden cross   £12
- vase (not exceeding 12″ × 8″ × 8″)   £25
- tablet for cremated remains (up to 21″ × 21″)   £44
- any other memorial, including inscription   £102
- additional inscription, added later   £24

Anything other than a simple headstone or inscription requires the granting of a faculty. The wording of an inscription must be approved by the incumbent; most will object to colloquialism and informal descriptions, and generally stipulate that any quotations are biblical or otherwise religious.

Municipal and private cemeteries are generally less rigorous in legis-lating about types of stone and wording of inscriptions; it is important to check out what limitations are imposed on memorials by the churchyard or cemetery before a burial takes place, although it may be the last thing in mind when arranging a funeral.

The funeral director is frequently involved in these arrangements, and will warn clients of any restrictions he or she knows about. Nevertheless, a recent change of incumbent in a parish church may result in a different interpretation of memorial guidelines, and it is important to tell the funeral director of the family's probable intentions regarding a memorial as soon as possible. Some funeral directors provide their own service of monumental masonry; almost all have contact with stonemasons whom they use as subcontractors.

Some crematoria now employ memorial consultants who, at the family's request, will make appointments to discuss various kinds of memorial with the relatives at a convenient time following the funeral. Bereaved families should beware of 'cold calling' memorial salespersons, who cull the local papers for bereavement notices and attempt to make doorstep sales.

Arranging for a memorial

The funeral director or monumental mason will normally apply to the church or cemetery authorities for permission to erect a memorial; a copy of the entry in the burial register or the deeds of the grave may be required before authority is given.

After a burial, several months should be allowed for settlement before any memorial is erected or replaced. Time should be taken in the consideration and purchase of a memorial; unsolicited memorial salesmen should be ignored. Names of established local firms of monumental masons can be obtained from the National Association of Memorial Masons★ or the Association of Burial Authorities.★

Do not, under any circumstances, order a memorial from any source before ascertaining what the burial ground regulations are.

The cost of memorials varies enormously, depending on the type of stone, size, ornamentation, finish and lettering. Before ordering a memorial, ask for a written estimate which states clearly the items and total cost, including any delivery or erection charges and cemetery fees. It is normal for the stonemason to ask for a 50 per cent deposit to be paid by the client on confirmation of the order: this may seem a lot, but if the client changes his or her mind, there is not much the mason can do with the already inscribed stone.

VAT is charged on the provision of a new headstone or on adding a new inscription to an old one; it is not levied on the removal and replacement of existing memorials. The cemetery fee for the erection of a memorial is also exempt from VAT.

Memorials online

With the rapid increase in the number of people who now have access to the Internet and email has come the development of an Internet memorial business. In addition to web sites giving information about grief support services, such as that of the London Bereavement Network,★ which includes details of services throughout the UK, there are sites which will help you develop your own web page, either for a fee of about £30 or for a donation. While these sites will last only as long as the relevant webmaster is in business, they provide the opportunity for posting a much fuller obituary than is possible in national or local papers, and at a fraction of the cost. Web sites may include photographs, video clips and music. For an example of the type of service available, check out *www.angelsonline.com*

Most providers are American, but fees can readily be paid by credit card. This is generally safe but users should take precautions. Look for 'secure' web sites (usually marked as such) and keep a record of emails and other transactions, or use traditional methods such as phone, fax or post to avoid giving card details electronically. Note that sites may change their content and locations frequently, and information may be inaccurate.

After cremation

About a week after a cremation has taken place, the crematorium will usually send a brochure to the next of kin explaining what kinds of memorials are available. These are all optional, are not covered by the fees paid for cremation, and are subject to the payment of VAT.

The most popular means of memorial at the crematorium is the 'Book of Remembrance'. Hand-lettered inscriptions in the book usually consist of the name, date of death, and a short epitaph; the charge depends on the length of the entry. The crematorium displays the book, open at the right page, on the anniversary of death or of the funeral: the relatives choose which they prefer. Some crematoria sell a miniature reproduction of the entry in the form of a card, or bound as a booklet, the price of which depends on the quality of the presentation.

Charges for the erection of memorial plaques or for inscriptions on panels in memorial passages, where available, vary greatly. Some municipal crematoria will allow no memorial other than the entry in the Book of Remembrance.

Some crematoria have a colonnade of niches for ashes called a columbarium; the ashes are either walled in by a plaque or left in an urn in the niche. Most of these are now full, and where there are spaces charges are high. Some new, private crematoria, however, have recently made extensive provision for these and similar memorials.

Other crematoria have memorial trees, or rose bushes; these are usually arranged in beds, where the memorial bush is chosen by the family, the ashes scattered around it, and a small plaque placed nearby. Costs vary, as does the length of time for which the crematorium will provide maintenance before another charge is made.

Charitable donations

An increasing amount of people ask family and friends to make donations to a nominated charity in memory of the deceased, and regard this as a fitting memorial for the person concerned. Usually, the funeral director will collect and forward donations to the appropriate charity, sending receipts to each donor and providing the charity and family with a list of donations received. The funeral director will not normally charge for this service.

Chapter 17

Away from home

As people move from place to place more often nowadays, they often express a wish to be buried or cremated in a district other than the one in which they died. In such cases, funeral arrangements have to be made in two places: where the death occurred, and where the funeral is to take place. Most funeral directors are accustomed to this, but if the distance involved is too great, the funeral director may subcontract arrangements at the other end to a colleague on the spot.

Bodies are usually conveyed by hearse within the UK, as this is normally the quickest and cheapest form of transport. It is quite possible to send a coffin by rail or air, but this is likely to be much more expensive: the coffin must be packed in a strong wooden crate and covered with hessian – this adds to the size and weight, and therefore to the cost. Charges vary according to distance and route covered, but airlines may charge double or treble the normal cargo rates, or may charge a special rate for carrying a coffin with a body inside.

The crated coffin must be accompanied by all the necessary documents for the funeral and the body must be embalmed if it is to be conveyed by any form of public transport. It is also normal practice to ensure that a body is embalmed before carrying it any considerable distance by hearse. Most funeral directors will deal with a distant funeral by accompanying the hearse and driver, and hiring bearers at the other end from a local colleague.

Registration must be effected in the registration district where the person died, and not where the funeral is to take place; it is, however, possible to give the information to a registrar in the funeral location, subject to the conditions in **Chapter 2**, 'Registering the death'.

Death abroad

When a British subject dies abroad, whether as a resident or as a visitor, the death must be registered where he or she died according to local regulations and customs. This is far from uncommon: in 1995, more than 1,300 British deaths abroad were reported to the Foreign Office. In many countries, the British consul can also register the death: this has the advantage that certified copies of the entry in the Register of Deaths can eventually be obtained from the General Register Office,★ just as if the death had been registered in the UK.

If such registration is required, an application form should be obtained, completed and returned to the Nationality and Passport Section of the Foreign and Commonwealth Office (FCO),★ together with the death certificate issued by the local authorities in the country concerned. If the consular office in the country where the death occurs is aware of the death, a separate document bearing a consular stamp is usually included with the package of documents accompanying the body. This document should also be sent with the application form. If the consular office where the death took place is not aware of the death, then the passport and birth certificate should be sent with the application as proof of UK citizenship; these will be returned to the applicant.

A consular fee is payable for the registration of the death in the UK, and a further fee is payable for each certificate issued at the time of registration; these fees vary periodically, and applicants should ask the FCO what fees are needed to accompany their application. This is a lengthy process, and considerable delay should be expected.

If such application is not made, there is no official record of the death in the UK. In this case, in order for the funeral to take place the registrar of the relevant district must be asked to supply a registrar's certificate confirming that death is not required to be registered, commonly called a 'certificate of no liability to register'. For this, a copy of the foreign death certificate, suitably translated into English (although many European countries now use a multi-lingual death certificate which does not need translation), must be supplied, giving the cause of death. The funeral director will normally be able to obtain both the translation and the certificate. Consular registration can take place after the funeral: a 'certificate of no liability to register' does not inhibit this process.

If someone dies while abroad, and their identity cannot be fully established after extensive investigation, the local officials will complete a death certificate with as much detail as they know, and eventually provide a funeral in accordance with the custom of the country where the death occurred.

Death at sea

When a death occurs on a foreign ship, it counts as a death abroad; the death must be recorded in the ship's log, and the port superintendent where the ship's crew are discharged must make enquiries into the cause of death.

When death occurs on a British-registered ship, the death is recorded in the captain's log, and all facts and particulars relating to the death must be recorded and delivered to the Registry of Shipping and Seamen★ on arrival at any port within or outside the UK. The master of any ship has the authority to decide whether, for health reasons, a body should be immediately disposed of at sea or kept for disposal later. As in most of these cases the death is unexpected, the body is usually kept in order to assist with a coroner's enquiry. Most cruise ships have mortuary facilities for cold storage of those who have died on board.

When a body is brought into a British port, the death must be reported to the coroner in whose jurisdiction the port is located. He or she may decide to order an enquiry, in which case the body cannot be moved without his or her consent. The registrar of the district in which the funeral is to take place must also issue a 'certificate of no liability to register', for which either a copy of the entry in the captain's log or a death certificate must be obtained. Copies of log entries can be obtained from the shipping company which owns the ship concerned, or the port superintendent where the body was brought ashore. Copies of the death certificate may be obtained from the Registry of Shipping and Seamen.★ This will normally all be dealt with by the funeral director.

Death in the air

When death occurs in an aircraft, the death must be registered in the country to which that aircraft belongs. At the next landing following the death, the captain must notify the local police authorities and the appropriate registration authority, which may not be in the same country as the one where the aircraft has landed. Subsequent action concerning arrangements for the body varies according to local regulations, but as far as relatives are concerned the procedure is the same as that for a death which occurs abroad. These arrangements can be extremely complicated, and will normally be dealt with by the funeral director in conjunction with a specialist repatriation service.

Returning a body from abroad

When someone dies abroad and the body is to be returned to the UK, the process is complex and expensive. Holiday or travel insurance which covers repatriation is essential, as the cost can run to several thousand pounds. Those who are travelling on package holidays should immediately contact their holiday representative: the biggest tour operators have proper procedures for handling bereavement. Further, tour operators belonging to ABTA subscribe to a code of conduct which commits them to assistance in many areas of bereavement, even where death occurs from an activity outside the normal holiday arrangements. They are also able to provide help with legal costs where necessary. Those travelling independently should ensure that their insurance covers repatriation, and be aware of the emergency telephone number on which to contact the insurance company or travel agency. Note that normal holiday insurance does not usually cover dangerous sports such as paragliding or scuba diving; additional cover must be taken out to cover such activities. For more information, see *The Which? Guide to Insurance*, available from Which? Books.*

The British Consul in the area will be able to advise, but will not be able to help financially. The consul may be some distance from where death occurred: in the Caribbean or Greek islands he or she may well not be on the same island. Independent travellers should also contact the local police or ambulance service as soon as possible. If there appears to be no one to advise, it would be wise to telephone a reputable funeral director in the UK to ask for advice and assistance; most funeral directors are experienced in these matters, and can turn to specialist repatriation services if they need help.

If the deceased had no insurance and the high cost of repatriation cannot be met, local cremation may be the only option available; it will almost certainly be the cheapest option. Provided a certificate of contents is obtained from the crematorium, the ashes can be brought back to the UK as hand luggage. This option, however, is not always available: most Muslim countries have no facilities for cremation, while in Nepal bodies are normally cremated on open-air funeral pyres, which may be found unacceptable.

The death must be registered in the country and area concerned, and death certificates and the doctor's medical certificate of the cause of death obtained. The local judicial authorities may want to investigate and, in any case, authority must be obtained from them to move the body out of their country. The body must be embalmed before it can be moved, and a certificate of embalming will be required. The body must be contained in a metal-lined coffin, which in turn must be covered with hessian and contained in a strong wooden crate. All necessary papers for customs clearance must be obtained, and arrangements made with an airline to convey the body to the UK – the usual method of repatriation.

Insurance companies will have contracts with repatriation services or firms of international funeral directors who will attend to all of this; if there is no insurance it is possible for relatives to attend to the matter, but specialist knowledge and a great deal of patience are required and the matter would be better entrusted to a UK funeral director. On arrival in the UK, customs clearance must be obtained; this may take several hours, but, once cleared, the body must be removed from the airport as soon as possible.

If death has occurred due to natural causes, the coroner will have only minimal involvement. If death is not due to natural causes, but is the result of an accident or criminal activity, the coroner in whose jurisdiction the airport lies will want to hold an inquest, and the body may not be moved from the mortuary until permission is given.

The registrar of the district in which the funeral is to take place must be informed, so that a 'certificate of no liability to register' can be issued. For this, evidence of death and the cause of death will be required.

Funerals involving burial

If the funeral is to involve burial, all the documents received with the coffin must be taken to the registrar in the district where the funeral will take place, with the relevant papers suitably translated. The

123

funeral director will normally attend to this, or the coroner's office may be able to help. The registrar will issue a 'certificate of no liability to register', which takes the place of the green certificate (see page 38) and is the only document required by burial authorities, whether a church or local authority.

Funerals involving cremation

If the funeral is to involve cremation, the local registrar must issue a certificate of no liability as in the case of burial, but considerable further paperwork is involved. Application must be made to the Home Office★ for authority to cremate; a certificate will be issued which will take the place of statutory **Forms B** and **C**. To obtain this, statutory **Form A** must be completed and signed, and taken to the Home Office with all documents received with the coffin: the foreign death certificate, embalming certificate, medical certificate of the cause of death, coroner's authority to remove the body from the country and, possibly, a 'freedom from infection' certificate. These may be sent or taken to the Home Office.★

Obviously this will be time-consuming and plans for the funeral must be adjusted accordingly. If sent by post, the envelope containing the papers should be marked 'Cremation papers: urgent'; it will be quicker to take the papers personally and wait while they are processed. Normally, the funeral director will attend to this.

All documents received from or returned by the Home Office should then be taken to the local registrar in order to obtain a 'certificate of no liability to register'; all these papers must then be submitted to the crematorium, although certain papers, such as copies of foreign death certificates, will probably be returned.

In some countries, the only form of death certificate issued is a carbon-copy or photocopy of the written entry in the local Register of Deaths. This presents problems to most UK registrars, who are required to see an 'original' death certificate. The funeral director can notify the registrar that this is the only document available.

When the coroner is involved

Repatriations invariably involve returning the body to the UK by air. If death appears to have been caused by something other than natural causes, the coroner of the district where the destination airport lies must be informed. He or she may order a post mortem and, if satisfied that death did occur from natural causes, will then issue the necessary documents: if the funeral involves burial, the coroner will authorise a 'certificate of no liability to register', which is all that is required; if cremation, he or she will issue the coroner's certificate for cremation, and the Home Office will not be involved at all.

If the coroner finds that death did not occur from natural causes, he or she will order an inquest to be held, the results of which may well be inconclusive due to the embalming or deterioration of the body and the inability to call witnesses. In this case, the funeral cannot be held until authority to do so is obtained from the coroner.

Sending a body abroad

When someone who has died in England or Wales is going to be buried or cremated in another country (including Scotland, Northern Ireland and the Channel Isles), permission must first be obtained from the local coroner. **Form 104** gives notice to a coroner of intention to remove a body from England, which will be supplied by the registrar or funeral director: usually the funeral director deals with this.

If the registrar knows before registration that the body is to be taken out of England, he or she will not issue a certificate for burial or cremation; if, however, such a certificate has already been issued, it must be sent to the coroner together with the 'out of England' form. Four clear days must normally elapse before the coroner gives permission on **Form 103**. However, in cases of urgency, a personal visit to the coroner's office with all necessary documentation and information concerning the death will, provided the coroner is satisfied, enable the form to be signed and the body removed immediately. If the coroner is already in the process of investigating the death, he or she will not release the body for removal from England until satisfied that it will not be required for further examination.

There are no legal restrictions on taking cremated remains out of the UK, but other countries may impose their own restrictions. For example, Italy is the most difficult: the ashes are treated exactly the same as a body, with all the same documents required, together with permission to import from the local prefect of police in the area of intended disposal. A hermetically sealed container is required, the sealing of which must have been witnessed by a representative of the consul. Greece treats ashes in the same way as an exhumed body, which may not be imported into the country until one year after death. France requires consular sealing of a hermetically sealed container bearing an engraved plate which gives the name of the deceased, date of death and death certificate number. India requires a High Commission permit. For all other countries, enquiries should be made at the relevant embassy or consulate.

Making the arrangements

Making the arrangements to take a body into another country for burial or cremation is an extremely complex matter and should not be contemplated without expert help. Generally, the body must be embalmed (there are few exceptions) and contained in a metal-lined coffin which is covered in hessian and strongly crated. All necessary freight documents must be completed, and a death certificate provided for UK customs clearance. Consular requirements of the destination country must be met, and all documents required must be translated and authenticated at the relevant consulate for a fee.

Consular regulations

Consular regulations vary, but usually only in certain respects; they also change frequently, so in every case enquiries should be made at the local consulate of the country concerned.

The requirements usually include:

- consular permission to take the body into the relevant country
- a copy of the certificate of death supplied by the registrar, suitably translated
- an official certificate stating the cause of death and a declaration that sanitary regulations for transporting the body will be met
- a certificate of embalming
- a declaration from the funeral director that the coffin contains only the body of the deceased and accompanying clothing and packing
- details of the route, flight number, and date of departure
- a 'freedom from infection' certificate (FFI)
- a certificate of exhumation and a copy of the Home Office licence to exhume, in the case of exhumed bodies

- a passport wherever it is necessary for the body to pass through another country on the way to its destination – this does not apply to air transport
- a consul representative's presence at the sealing of the coffin/crate.

In addition, the consulate will also provide information about formalities that will be required on arrival of the body, and what arrangements must be made beforehand.

Burial at sea

Burial at sea may be requested by anyone; it is relatively unusual, fairly complicated and very expensive. All materials disposed of at sea require a licence under the Food and Environmental Protection Act 1985 (modified by the Environmental Protection Act 1990); this includes bodies, but in order to minimise stress to the bereaved, the government will, in place of issuing a licence, accept written notification from a funeral director that he or she intends to bury a body at sea.

The letter must contain the name and address of the applicant (normally the funeral director), the date and time period for which permission is required, and the information that a human body is to be disposed of at sea. This should be sent to The Sea Fisheries Inspectorate.★

Time must be allowed for a reply, and other documentation must be gathered. Registration must take place in the district where death occurred, although information may be given at any register office (see **Chapter 2**). An application must be made to the coroner on **Form 104** to remove the body from England. A copy of the death certificate will be required, and a declaration as to whether death was caused by an infectious disease. The coroner will give permission on **Form 103** for the body to be removed and buried at sea.

Permission from the District Inspectorate of Fisheries must be obtained – the Sea Fisheries Inspectorate★ will advise on this – and will be given only for a very small number of specified locations, almost always outside the three-mile limit.

The coffin must be made from solid wood, have many holes drilled in it, and contain suitable heavy weights to ensure it will sink. Where such burials are preceded by a church service, the coffin should be covered with a pall.

Arrangements for a suitable vessel must be made, allowing for the fact that not only must a heavy coffin be carried and lowered into the sea in a respectful way, but also that a number of passengers will want to accompany it on the boat. Local harbour masters can be a source of relevant information; generally, however, all arrangements can be made by an experienced funeral director.

No documents are required for scattering or burying ashes at sea.

Death while in the armed forces

If a member of the forces dies serving abroad, the Ministry of Defence normally allows the next of kin the following choice:

- a funeral overseas with two people from the UK (normally the next of kin) attending, all at public expense
- repatriation of the body where practicable at public expense to a funeral director in the UK chosen by the family. Once the body has reached the funeral director, the family becomes responsible for the funeral. The Ministry of Defence provides the coffin and a grant of £1,025 towards burial, or £625 towards cremation.

If a serviceman or -woman dies in the UK, the next of kin can choose to have:

- **a military funeral at public expense** This will be arranged and paid for by the Ministry of Defence, provided it takes place near to where the death occurred. (Exceptionally, because military funerals cannot be arranged in Northern Ireland, a member of the forces dying there can be buried anywhere in the UK at public expense).
- **a private funeral with limited military assistance** The Ministry of Defence pays for the coffin and the conveyance of the body some distance from the place of death to a funeral director chosen by the family. Once the body has reached the funeral director's premises, the family is responsible for the funeral. The Ministry of Defence pays a grant towards the cost of the funeral: £1,025 in the case of burial, £625 in the case of cremation.
- **a private-expense funeral** In this case, the next of kin claim the body and make all the arrangements privately (including the provision of a coffin). The Ministry of Defence makes the following allowances: £1,175 towards burial, £750 in the case of cremation.

A member of the forces who dies while serving may be buried in a military cemetery by consultation with the appropriate cemetery authorities. This will be arranged at public expense if there is a military cemetery near to where the death occurred.

If someone who was receiving a war disablement pension dies as a result of that disablement or was drawing a constant attendance allowance, the Department of Social Security may pay for a simple funeral. The next of kin should contact the local war pensioners' welfare office straight away, before any formal arrangements are made.

Chapter 18

The grief process

Death alters the course of daily life for all those closest to the person who had died. If someone close to you has died, you must accept that things will change, whether the change is small or immense. Something irreversible has happened and your life must now follow a different course. You will face various experiences which will affect you in certain ways until, having worked through them, you arrive at a point where your life is once again moving steadily in a positive direction.

Normal grief

Bereavement is a very complex issue; this short chapter describes many of the phases that you may encounter when recently bereaved. Any description of reactions to grief has to be simplified because of the enormous variation from person to person in coping with the situation. Nevertheless, the considerable amount of study which has taken place over the last 25 years has revealed much that is common to the great majority of people.

There is nothing unusual about grieving: it is 'normal' and most people will make a 'normal' recovery without a great deal of assistance. Some, however, get stuck somewhere in the process of recovery and need help; others (fortunately, only a few) are so affected by their bereavement that the grief process gets out of hand. In such cases, treatment as well as assistance is needed, counsel as well as care. The normal grief processes only are covered in this section to help you understand how you may be feeling.

Most of the time, bereavement causes a great deal of pain; many people do not acknowledge this, fearing that they will be marked out as weak and abnormal. Family and friends will often avoid people who have lost partners, children or close friends, usually because they are embarrassed and do not know what to say. They excuse their feelings of embarrassment and helplessness by saying things like: 'Grief is a very private affair. I don't want to intrude.' So the bereaved are often deserted just when they need most support, which leads them to believe that it is their pain and tears that cause others to shun them; they therefore make determined efforts to 'be strong' and suppress their natural emotional responses. More than anything else, this hinders recovery from grief.

Reactions to grief

When loss has occurred and the bereaved person has been diverted from the accustomed course of life, a number of psychological forces come into effect. The different stages of grief that a person may go through include shock, sorrow, anger, apathy and depression, before the process of recovery can begin. Not everyone experiences all of these emotions, and some stages may last longer than others. In other words, everyone is different.

Shock: the primary experience

The initial effect of bereavement is shock. There is a numbness in which the rest of the world often seems to recede, leaving the bereaved person in mental limbo; a common feeling is of the world carrying on but the person no longer feeling part of it. This leads almost immediately into a stage of denial – the strong feeling that death cannot possibly have occurred, that the bereaved is dreaming, that the doctors have made a mistake. This begins at the moment of loss and has its major impact during the first two to three days. At this stage, people can be very susceptible; this should be recognised and great care taken when an important decision has to be made – especially the arrangements for the funeral. Dates and times often have to be decided upon quickly, but sufficient time should be allowed before the funeral to avoid making the wrong decisions in haste.

When death occurs after a long illness, or where there was ill-feeling between the deceased and the bereaved, the initial response is a feeling of relief: the tension is at last over and done with. This may be accompanied almost at once by a sense of guilt for feeling relieved – talking about this to a sensible and trustworthy friend will help.

Sorrow: the underlying experience

Shock often overlaps with or is followed by feelings of sorrow – the sadness which develops as the person becomes aware that an irreversible loss has occurred. Sorrow and pining can have the effects of physical pain, often made worse by the belief that one is supposed to 'be strong' and not show any undue signs of emotional disturbance. At this point, the bereaved person needs to be free to express grief with the support of others who will not be embarrassed or try to suppress the person's tears. In order to make a good recovery, the bereaved person needs to feel this pain, express it and work through it in ways which are appropriate to his or her personality.

But initial sorrow is often accompanied by unreasonable guilt. People often feel guilty because they think they could have done more than they did – had they done more, perhaps the deceased person would not have died – and much reassurance and patience are called for. This often leads to people 'bargaining' with God or with life in general (for example, by promising to be good if only they can wake up to find that it was all a bad dream). The only way to help someone going through these emotions is to root the person firmly in reality, to talk about the death and to have the person visit the body in a chapel of rest, thus allowing a gradual acceptance of the situation to come about in a way that can be coped with.

The acute stage of this phase does not usually last for very long, and is sometimes over in two or three weeks. The sorrow will persist, but will generally subside into a numbing ache. The guilt (real or imagined) may well last for a long time.

Anger: the developing experience

Many people get very angry when bereaved, usually in an irrational manner. There is anger with God (for letting death happen), with friends and family (for not understanding or for not being bereaved themselves), with themselves (for not coping) and with the deceased (for having died and left them). Sometimes the anger comes before the sorrow and guilt, sometimes after, and is often compounded by a strong and irrational resentment and a certain amount of aggression (depending on the person's personality – a very mild person is unlikely to become extremely aggressive). Friends need a great deal of patience: they should let the person cool down, then listen to the anger without being defensive or argumentative.

This stage of the grief process can last from a few days to several months. It may continue to simmer in the background for a long time, resulting in outbursts of irrational anger at unexpected times. Those on the receiving end should remember that the anger is not directed at them and try not to feel injured or aggrieved.

Apathy, depression and recovery

When the anger calms down, a state of apathy often develops. The bereaved person displays indifference to what is going on round about him or her and may show a considerable reluctance to make decisions. Patience and encouragement are needed continuously.

Or there may be feelings of depression. Most people can work through these normal feelings of depression with the support of friends and family; however, this support should not be allowed to turn into an unhealthy dependence on the help of others – it is important to encourage people by doing things *with* them rather than *for* them, so that they will once again be able to do things for themselves. Occasionally, depression can degenerate into acute depression, where professional assistance is called for.

Gradually, even when the pain of bereavement has been acute, a sense of acceptance grows and the bereaved person once again begins to take an interest in life. When it becomes possible for the person to make positive plans for the future and again find pleasure in everyday experience, the bereaved person is well on the way to recovery. Life will never be the same again, but it can now be lived in a normal, healthy manner.

Other common reactions

Shock can also have physical effects, leading to quite genuine symptoms. These are often not recognised as being part of the normal grief process and, as a result, many recently bereaved people worry that they have a physical illness on top of the burden of bereavement.

Headaches are common, as are a continuously dry mouth, weakness, breathlessness, oversensitivity to noise, tightness in the chest and throat, a hollow feeling in the stomach, giddiness and nausea. Hair loss may also occur. Some people lose weight, others put it on; some people are constantly tired, even when they have had sufficient sleep and food.

There are often real feelings of fear, sometimes based on the person's anxiety that he or she will not be able to cope. Absentmindedness and lack of ability to concentrate on anything for very long are also common: sometimes people forget what they were saying in mid-sentence. Memory is frequently affected: facts, names, experiences, all well known, cannot be brought to mind when needed, which can be very upsetting.

All of these are quite normal experiences, and recognising them as such will greatly assist you to live through them and come to terms with the reality of the bereavement which has occurred.

On the way to recovery

In practice, of course, it is seldom as simple as this. Some people do not appear to go through any of the emotional phases listed above, while others pass from feeling to feeling, only to repeat the process a few weeks later. Realising that there is no one certain way that you're *supposed* to feel will help you on your way to recovery.

Chapter 19

Child and cot deaths

Every year, about 8,000 babies in the UK die within the first month of life, or are stillborn; one couple out of every 500 has suffered this form of bereavement. Yet only recently has this experience been recognised as real bereavement; previously, parents who had lost new-born babies were expected to recover quickly from their loss.

Recent research has indicated, however, that mourning lasts longer among bereaved parents than in widows or widowers; in a recent survey of parents who had lost babies in the first few months of life, two-thirds of those interviewed felt that their main need was to have their baby recognised as a real person, and not as 'something that could be replaced'.

Memorials

Mourning involves memories, and when a small baby dies, memories are few. Until very recently, it used to be felt that the less the parents knew about the dead baby, the less they would grieve; the mother was often sedated, and the dead child whisked away before she or the father could see it. Relatives were advised to dispose of any potential reminders: baby clothes were removed, pram and cot disposed of and toys given away or carefully hidden. This deprived the parents of almost all the grounds of memory, thus making it almost impossible for them to find a degree of healing through mourning.

Active contact with the dead baby greatly helps to make it a real person to bereaved parents, and supplies at least some of the memories they need. Mothers are more often encouraged to hold their dead baby, and to wash and dress it. Photographs can provide memories and confirm the reality of a child's existence, thus providing a source of comfort. Expensive equipment is unnecessary: a simple photograph will do. A lock of hair can be kept, or a little down snipped from the baby's head and kept in a transparent envelope. Handprints or foot-prints can be taken with washable ink pads, and suitably mounted. A toy or two intended for the baby can be placed with it in the coffin.

The funeral

Parents who have lost babies or small children should be encouraged to resist the temptation to get the funeral over with as soon as possible. The funeral service is one of the few things which bereaved parents can arrange for their babies, and as much time and thought as possible should go into discussing the details. The Foundation for the Study of Infant Deaths (FSID)★ publishes a leaflet, *Information for parents following the unexpected death of their baby*, which contains lots of helpful advice. The funeral will cause pain, but this pain is a necessary part of the healing and recovery process.

Many, probably most, funeral directors will make no charge for arranging the funeral of a baby or small child; funeral arrangements, services of staff, use of the chapel of rest, an appropriate coffin and a hearse or estate car will normally be provided free. If elaborate funeral arrangements are requested, such as a solid wood coffin or cars for mourners, these will have to be paid for. Many hospitals now make provision for the reverent disposal of miscarriages or stillbirths, with a simple funeral service often taking place in the hospital chapel or local crematorium.

Most crematoria do not charge for the cremation of children under the age of one year: it should be noted that some crematoria are unable to provide cremated remains for disposal afterwards, as the cremation process is usually total, leaving no ashes for disposal.

Many cemeteries also make no charge for the burial of infants under one year, and fees for burial in churchyards are frequently waived. Headstones or other memorial stones will, however, be subject to the same fees as adults'.

Care agencies

A number of care agencies exist for the sole purpose of offering help and support to those who have lost babies and small children. Compassionate Friends★ is one such society whose valuable function is not always recognisable from its name.

Chapter 20

Probate, pensions and property

None of the property of the deceased should be sold, nor, strictly speaking, given away until probate has been granted. Probate is the official validation and approval of a will, and application must be made to the nearest probate court for approval before the intentions of the deceased can be put into practice. This will take at least several weeks. If the deceased left no will, 'letters of administration' must be applied for; this will take longer. For further details of how to administer an estate, see *Wills and Probate*, available from Which? Books.*

Probate is not normally required if the value of the estate totals less than £5,000; the guidelines of the probate court allow them to dispense with probate for sums in excess of this if the settlement of the estate is straightforward. If there are disputes about the settlement of the estate, or possible future complications can be foreseen, then probate should always be applied for.

Until probate or letters of administration are granted, the deceased's executor must inform the bank, which will stop payment of all cheques and banker's orders; however, the major banks will generally release funds to pay the funeral account if presented with a legitimate account from a funeral director. The post office, building society, or any other institution where the deceased had an account must also be notified; any savings will be temporarily frozen. The tax inspector must also be informed that the death has occurred.

After the grant of probate or letters of administration, the executor settles all debts, obtains payment of any life insurance policy, and transfers the ownership of any house, shares, or other property the deceased may have had.

The Scottish equivalent of probate is *confirmation*; the *appointment of an executor-dative* is the equivalent of letters of administration.

Pensions and tax

All pension books and allowance books of the deceased must be returned, either to the DSS or to the issuing office quoted in the payment book; notes of the pension and/or allowance numbers should be carefully kept. If there are any uncashed orders, they must not be cashed after death, even if signed. Any unpaid amounts should be claimed when the book is returned. Any outstanding pension or allowance payments must be specifically claimed by the executors: they will not be paid automatically.

To get any unpaid portions of a war pension, write to the War Pensions Agency★ and claim the amount due, quoting the pension number.

If the deceased had been an officer in one of the armed forces and a pension or allowance was being paid on the basis of war service, the next payment that comes will have to be returned, uncashed, to the issuing office. Send with it a note of the place and date of death, and claim any amount that has become due in the period from the last payment to the death.

If income tax was being deducted from the dead person's salary under the pay-as-you-earn (PAYE) scheme, a refund of tax may be due, depending on the date of death and the tax paid up to then. You will have to apply to the inspector of taxes for the area where the deceased's tax affairs were dealt with; if no one contacts him or her about a refund, the inspector of taxes will not do anything about it. (The executors will hear from the collector of taxes if there is any tax to be paid.)

A widow gets a bereavement allowance (as well as a single person's allowance) to set against her income from the date of her husband's death to the end of the tax year in which he died and for the following tax year (unless she remarries before the new tax year begins). The amount of the widow's bereavement allowance is equal to the difference between the single person's allowance and the married man's allowance.

When independent taxation for husbands and wives was introduced at the beginning of the tax year 1990–1, the system of allowances changed. If a wife dies the husband carries on getting the married couple's tax allowance for the year on top of his own personal allowance. If a husband dies, his widow can get any of the married couple's allowance not used against his income up to the date of his death; and after his death she will get the widow's bereavement allowance plus the additional personal allowance if she has a child living with her, all in addition to her own personal allowance.

The Inland Revenue leaflet **IR91**, *A guide for widows and widowers*, is also helpful.

Home and possessions

Responsibility for a house or flat may need to be transferred to the name of another person. Relatives who were living with the deceased in rented accommodation should seek advice about their rights from the local Citizens Advice Bureau★ or solicitor.

Depending on income and circumstances, a widow or widower may be eligible for Housing Benefit paid through the local authority to assist with rent or council tax. DSS leaflet **GL16**, *Help with your rent*, can be obtained from Benefits Agencies and from some post offices; a more detailed explanation is given in leaflet **RR2**, *Housing benefit and council tax benefit*.

If the telephone was in the name of the deceased, the telephone company should be notified, and the service transferred to another name or terminated. A request should be made for the account up to the time of death to be rendered, so that the debt can be paid from the estate. Similarly, requests should be made to gas and electricity suppliers for meters to be read and accounts submitted; these accounts must also be transferred to another name.

Should a home help or meals-on-wheels have been supplied, the local authority social services department must be notified, and any loaned aid or appliance returned. Library books, records, cassettes and video tapes should be returned to the respective libraries. If a house or flat has to be cleared quickly, any furniture not required can be offered to a local dealer or put in an auction sale; a number of second-hand or antique dealers offer house clearance services – see local advertisements or *Yellow Pages*. The agreement should ensure that the house is left completely empty, and clean. Sometimes, especially after the sudden death of someone who lived alone, there is an urgent need for drastic cleaning of floors, carpets, bedding, furniture or curtains. Specialist contract cleaners offer such a service: again, see the local telephone book or *Yellow Pages*; funeral directors can often advise.

Local charity shops are glad to receive saleable items, although they must be delivered to the charity concerned at the donor's expense. If the local authority refuse department has to make a special collection, a charge may be made for this service. When a death is announced in local papers, second-hand clothing dealers sometimes call and offer to buy the deceased's clothes: this is an easy way to get rid of unwanted items, but very little will be offered for them. Check all pockets, bags, cases etc. before disposing of them. Other unwanted possessions can also be advertised for sale locally, offered to a dealer or second-hand shop, or given to a charity.

Papers

Various documents will need to be sorted out and examined, and action taken about them. The deceased's medical card should be taken to the registrar when registering the death; if this was not done, it should be sent to the registrar as soon as possible. A rail season ticket should be taken to the station where it was issued, together with proof of death or probate, and a refund claimed. There is no refund for unused railcards. London Underground or bus season tickets may be surrendered at any Underground station, or posted to the commercial office of London Regional Transport.★ A refund may be made from the last day of use if a death certificate is produced, otherwise from the date of surrender. Refunds are made to the widow or widower with no formality; an executor may claim the refund on production of proof of probate or letters of administration, or on producing a solicitor's letter authorising payment.

Passports should be returned to the Passport Office,★ or to any of the regional passport offices, together with a letter of explanation. If requested, passports will be returned after cancellation. Joint passports must be suitably amended by the Passport Office.

If the deceased owned a car, once the new ownership of the car has been settled, the top part of the registration document should be given to the new owner/keeper, and the bottom part sent to the Driver and Vehicle Licensing Agency (DVLA),★ so that the change of ownership can be recorded and a new registration document issued. The deceased's car insurance company should be notified immediately.

If a widow, widower or partner is now the sole occupant of the house or flat, a rebate on council tax should be applied for.

For all other insurance policies in the name of the deceased, the relevant companies should be notified, the policies cancelled or amended, and any appropriate refunds claimed.

Claiming money due

Clubs and associations to which the dead person belonged should be told of the death and any unwanted subscriptions cancelled. There may be a refund to claim on unexpired memberships.

To claim on a life insurance policy, send the policy to the company together with the standard death certificate. A policy made 'in trust' for the widow/widower or other named beneficiary bypasses probate, and payment can be made to the beneficiary straight away. In all other cases, payment may be delayed until probate is granted. If this is more than two months after the date of death, the insurance company must add interest, at the current market rate, from then until the payment is made.

A number of employers have a life insurance scheme that pays out a lump sum on the death of an employee. And most company pension schemes provide either a cash sum or a pension (sometimes both) for dependants. Find out from the dead person's last employers whether any such payments are now due.

Various societies, professional bodies, trade unions and ex-service organisations run benevolent schemes for the dependants of their members or of people who qualify within the scope of the organisation. The bereaved person should get in touch with the secretary of any organisation related to his or her late spouse's activities to find out what benevolent schemes might be available.

Chapter 21

Pensions and other state benefits

Following the death of a spouse or close relative, you may become eligible for certain payments from the state.

The Benefits Agency administers all Social Security benefits. Explanatory leaflets for different categories of people – for example, on widow's benefits – are available without charge at any local office of the Benefits Agency.* (A list of some relevant leaflets is given on pages 158–9.) It is crucial to note that these leaflets are updated at irregular intervals, and information contained in them may change considerably from one edition to another. Please see the important note at the end of this chapter, and ensure that you always have the latest edition of the leaflet you want. You can ask the Benefits Agency if all the information in it is correct and up to date.

Some benefits are paid only to the dependants of those who had paid, or had credited to them, National Insurance contributions during their lifetime.

You are not expected to know what contributions have been paid or credited when you apply for any benefits. The DSS keeps records of everyone's contributions.

The number of contributions required varies according to the type of benefit claimed. When the number of contributions does not qualify for the full amount of certain benefits, a reduced rate may be paid.

If you need to find out more about claiming any benefits after someone has died abroad, write to the Overseas Branch of the Department of Social Security.*

Help with funeral expenses

If you do not have enough money to pay for the funeral, and you or you and your partner are getting Income Support, Income-based Jobseeker's Allowance, Working Families' Tax Credit, Disability Working Allowance, Council Tax Benefit or Housing Benefit, and it is reasonable for you to take responsibility for the funeral costs, you may be able to get a payment from the Social Fund to help with the cost. The necessary cost of specified services may be met, including burial or cremation costs, plus up to £600 for other funeral expenses. This is to include provision of a simple coffin and gown, removal of the deceased from the place of death to the funeral director's premises (up to a distance of 50 miles), and church, minister's and organist's fees. The Social Fund will not pay for newspaper announcements, the burial of cremated remains (ashes), any memorials or flowers for the funeral (unless there is money available from the balance of the £600 allowance after all necessary fees have been paid).

It is considered reasonable for you to pay for the cost of the funeral if you are the partner of the person who has died, or if you are a close relative or friend of the person if they did not have a partner. Should the person who has died have a parent or children who are not receiving any of the qualifying benefits, the DSS will normally consider it reasonable for that person/those people to pay for the cost of the funeral.

If you qualify to receive payment from the Social Fund, and you or you and your partner together have savings over £500 (£1,000 for those aged 60 and over), this is taken into account. How much you get also depends on certain other funds which become available following the death, such as a life insurance policy, and any other money which is available for the funeral from other sources. If the person who died had a pre-paid funeral plan, payment from the Social Fund will only be paid for those necessary elements of the funeral not covered by the plan.

A funeral payment made by the Social Fund will have to be paid back from the estate of the person who has died, should there be any money available. The law requires that funeral expenses must be paid before anything else is paid from the estate. The home occupied by the partner of the person who has died, or personal possessions left to relatives, are not counted as part of the estate. You can find out more about funeral payments from the Social Fund in leaflet **SB16**.

Claims should be made on Form **SF200**, available from the Benefits Agency or funeral directors, which should be accompanied by a copy of the funeral director's account. Completed forms must be sent to one of the DSS offices dealing with Social Fund claims, or taken to the local Benefits Agency. Pre-paid envelopes may be supplied with the SF200 pack, but are also obtainable from any post office. Currently, claims must be made within three months of the funeral.

As both benefits and the means of claiming them have changed several times at short notice recently, it is most important to check current arrangements with the Social Fund office at the local Benefits Agency, preferably before finalising funeral arrangements. This may be the last thing you feel like doing, but it is important if financial embarrassment is to be avoided.

Details following on pages 147–53 relate mostly to widows, with the exception of 'Widowers and SERPs' on page 151; the section titled 'Other state benefits' is applicable to both men and women.

Widow's benefit

Widow's benefit is a term used by the Department of Social Security for payments to which a woman may become entitled following her husband's death. A widow qualifies only if her husband's National Insurance contribution record satisfies the appropriate conditions; her own contributions do not count. (There is no equivalent benefit for widowers.)

A woman can claim widow's benefit only if she was married to a man at the date of his death. If the marriage had been annulled or dissolved by divorce, the woman is not regarded as his lawful widow. But if the couple were in the process of getting divorced, the woman is deemed to have been married up to the point of the decree absolute. If she marries again while under 60, she loses her widow's benefit from her previous marriage.

A widow does not apply specifically for any one benefit but makes her claim on a detailed form (Form **BW1**), available at any office of the Benefits Agency, or by applying for it on the form certifying that death has been registered (**BD8**) as supplied free by the registrar. On form **BW1** she is asked to give particulars of herself and her late husband and of any dependent children.

If she can send her marriage and birth certificates too, this will help to speed up the process. However, it is not necessary to obtain replacement certificates if the originals can not be found.

It is most important that this form is sent off as soon as possible, advisedly not later than three months after her husband's death, in order not to lose any of the benefits. Claimants should not delay because they are waiting for probate, which may take several months, but make an initial claim as soon as possible.

A widow who qualifies for benefit can opt to be paid by a book of weekly orders, cashable at a post office, or to receive payments made four-weekly or quarterly in arrears directly into a bank or Girobank account, or a national savings bank or building society investment account. She specifies her choice when filling out application form BW1. Weekly orders are valid for three months; if not cashed within that time, a replacement order must be requested. The benefit of an order not cashed within 12 months is lost.

Widow's benefit is not affected by any earnings a widow may have or income from investments. It is, however, subject to income tax and may be affected by other Social Security benefits payable to her or similar payments out of public funds, such as a War Widow's Pension or a training allowance.

If her late husband's contributions were insufficient for her to receive the full, or any, widow's benefit, she will be informed in writing. She has a right of appeal to the Social Security appeal tribunal if she disagrees with the decision. This is explained in the notification, and a Citizens Advice Bureau★ can be asked about the procedure.

If a widow under 60 remarries she loses all entitlement to widow's benefits based on her previous husband's contribution record. A widow under 60 also loses her widow's benefits if she lives with a man as his wife, but can claim again once the cohabitation ends.

Social Security benefits are reviewed by the government at least once a year, and recently benefits and qualifying conditions have been changed at short notice. The current amounts for the benefits described in the following pages are on pages 156–8. It is, however, important to check the current position at the local Benefits Agency.

Widow's Payment
A widow under the age of 45 or whose husband was not getting a retirement pension when he died may get a tax-free lump sum of £1,000 (1999/2000), provided his National Insurance contributions record entitles her to it.

Widow's Pension
A widow who is over 45 but under pensionable age and who has no dependent children may receive a weekly pension in addition to Widow's Payment, depending on her husband's contribution record.

Widowed Mother's Allowance
A widow who is under 60 with one or more dependent children, or who is pregnant with her late husband's baby, will not receive Widow's Pension, but will instead be eligible to receive Widowed Mother's Allowance. As well as receiving a weekly sum for herself, she will also receive an additional allowance for each child under school-leaving age, or who is under 19 and a full-time student or apprentice, or whose schooling or apprenticeship has been interrupted because of illness. A widow can claim the extra allowance only for a child who was or would have been treated as part of her late husband's family, and normally only for a child living with her.

A widow continues to receive the widowed mother's personal allowance if any child over 16 but under 19 who has left school is still living with her; she does not receive an additional allowance for the child. A widow who is under 45 at the time when her children cease to qualify her for Widowed Mother's Allowance then receives nothing. A widow who by that time is over 45 and under 60 may receive the appropriate Widow's Pension for her age at that time.

Widow over 60
A widow who is over 60 but under 65 whose husband was not getting Retirement Pension may be eligible for Widow's Payment together with either Widow's Pension or Retirement Pension. If her husband had been receiving Retirement Pension she will not be eligible to receive Widow's Payment, but may be eligible for either Widow's Pension or Retirement Pension. In both cases, the Retirement Pension will normally be paid.

A widow who is over 65 whose husband had not been receiving Retirement Pension may be eligible for Widow's Payment and Retirement Pension; if her husband had been receiving Retirement Pension she will not receive Widow's Payment, but may be eligible for Retirement Pension.

A widow who is over 60 with a dependent child may be eligible for Widow's Payment (provided her husband had not been receiving Retirement Pension) and Widowed Mother's Allowance or Retirement Pension. Normally the Retirement Pension will be paid.

If a woman is 60 or over at the time of her husband's death and they had both been drawing the Retirement Pension, she can apply for her Retirement Pension to be changed to the rate for a widow. She may also be entitled to extra basic pension if her husband had deferred his retirement until after he was 65. In addition, she will receive half of any graduated pension he was getting.

If a widow is already drawing a Retirement Pension based on her own contributions, but a pension based on her late husband's contributions would be at a higher rate than her own, she may apply for her pension to be replaced by one based on his.

Widow under 60 without dependent children

The pension a widow receives depends on her age at the time of her husband's death. (Different rules apply for deaths before April 1988.) If a woman is under 45 when her husband dies, she does not receive a Widow's Pension.

A woman who was 45 or over but under 55 when her husband died is eligible to receive a Widow's Pension calculated on a sliding scale according to her age. This scale starts at 30 per cent of the standard rate for a woman aged 45 at that time and increases in seven per cent steps, so that a widow aged 54 when her husband died is eligible to receive 93 per cent of the standard rate. A widow who is 55 or over but under 60 at the time of her husband's death may receive the full standard rate of the basic pension.

Age-related Widow's Pension

The weekly rates for age-related Widow's Pension from April 1999 are listed below. Those receiving age-related Widow's Pension *before* 11 April 1988 should refer to the ages in brackets:

Age 54 (49).....£62.08   Age 49 (44).....£38.72
Age 53 (48).....£57.41   Age 48 (43).....£34.04
Age 52 (47).....£52.73   Age 47 (42).....£29.37
Age 51 (46).....£48.06   Age 46 (41).....£24.70
Age 50 (45).....£43.39   Age 45 (40).....£20.03

These amounts are likely to change annually; the amount and the qualifying conditions may change more frequently at short notice.

See leaflets **NP45** and **NP46** for further details, ensuring that you have the most recent edition, and leaflet **GL23** (which replaced the earlier **NI196**) for the current benefit rates.

SERPS or State Earnings Related Pensions

In addition to the standard Widow's Pension, a widow may also receive an additional pension based on her husband's earnings as an employed person from April 1978. This pension will be worked out according to a sliding scale revised annually, and published in DSS leaflets **NP45** and **NP46**. If her husband was a member of a contracted-out occupational pension scheme, part of his widow's additional pension will be payable by that scheme.

A widow can inherit the whole of her late husband's basic and SERPS pension. If she is entitled to a Retirement Pension based on her own contributions, she can add the two Retirement Pensions together. The sum of the basic pensions is, however, limited to the full rate of the basic pension for a single person, and the sum of the SERPS pensions to the maximum that a single contributor could have earned from April 1978.

A woman who is not yet drawing Retirement Pension when her husband dies may qualify for a Widow's Pension, even if she goes on working. Once she has retired, or reached the age of 65, she may inherit half her husband's graduated pension to add to her Retirement Pension as well as any graduated pension of her own.

Widowers and SERPs

A man whose wife dies when they are both over retirement age can draw a pension derived partly from her contribution record and partly from his own, in exactly the same way as a widow can do, up to the same maximum.

151

War Widow's Pension

A widow whose husband had been in the armed forces and whose death could be attributed to military service, or who had been drawing war pension constant attendance allowance, should write to the War Pensions Agency★ explaining the circumstances fully, and asking if she is entitled to a War Widow's Pension.

Contribution requirements

The requirements for Widow's Payment are that her late husband must have paid at least 25 Class 1, 2 or 3 contributions prior to age 65 before 6 April 1975, or, after 6 April 1975, he must have paid contributions in any one tax year on wages of at least 25 times the lower earnings limit for that year.

The requirements of Widow's Pension and Widowed Mother's Allowance are that her late husband must have had either one qualifying year since 6 April 1975 derived from actual payments of Class 1, 2 or 3 National Insurance contributions, or have paid 50 flat-rate contributions at any time before that date. For the whole of the standard rate to be paid, the husband must have had qualifying years for about 90 per cent of the years in his working life.

The husband's working life is normally taken to be the number of complete tax years in the period from 6 April before his 16th birthday to 5 April before his death, or before he reached the age of 65 if earlier. If he was already contributing to the insurance scheme before 5 July 1948, however, the period will count from the tax year in which he entered insurance or 6 April 1936, whichever is later. If he was over 16 on 5 July 1948 and entered insurance on or after that date, the period for the calculation of his working life will begin on 6 April 1948.

The number of years required for a standard rate of basic pension is calculated as follows:

	number of years required
less than 10 years in working life	number of years of working life, minus 1
11–20 years in working life	number of years of working life, minus 2
21–30 years in working life	number of years of working life, minus 3

31–40 years in working life	number of years of working life, minus 4
over 41 years in working life	number of years of working life, minus 5

If the husband had not paid enough years of contribution, his widow will be eligible for a pension reduced in proportion to the number of years of contributions paid, as long as at least a quarter of the number of qualifying years has been achieved.

Widows and National Insurance contributions

A woman who, immediately before her husband died, had full liability for National Insurance contributions (that is, she was required to pay standard-rate Class 1 contributions when employed and Class 2 contributions when self-employed) continues to do so as a widow.

However, if she was paying reduced-rate Class 1 contributions when employed immediately prior to the date her husband died, she continues to have reduced liability while she gets Widow's Benefit. If she does not receive Widow's Benefit, she will have reduced liability until the end of the tax year (5 April) in which her husband died if he died before 1 October, or until the end of the following tax year if he died on or after 1 October. If she changes from reduced-rate to full-rate liability at any time, she cannot then change back.

Reduced liability is lost if, for any two whole consecutive tax years since 6 April 1978, the widow has not been liable to pay Class 1 National Insurance contributions as an employed earner, and has not been self employed. Once this test cannot be satisfied, full liability is automatically in force from the end of the two-year period. This applies to both married women and widows. There is no liability for a woman to pay any National Insurance contributions after she reaches the age of 60, although this may change in the future.

Leaflet **CA09** gives full details of the contribution position of widows, and how payment of full or reduced contributions may affect entitlement to National Insurance benefits. A copy of the leaflet is issued to newly widowed women; any woman in doubt about her pension can ask the staff at her local Social Security or Benefits Agency office for further information and advice. If there is a significant gap in her recent contributions record, she may be able to remedy this by making voluntary (Class 3) contributions now.

Other state benefits

If your income and savings are below certain levels you may be able to claim benefits to top up your income. Advice can be obtained from agencies such as the Citizens Advice Bureau,★ as well as the Benefits Agency.★

Income Support

If you don't work or work for fewer than 16 hours a week and your savings total less than £8,000, you can claim Income Support if your weekly income is below a specified amount. This varies depending on your circumstances, i.e. your age, whether you have dependent children and, if so, how old they are, whether you are disabled or suffer from a chronic illness, whether you have a mortgage to pay and so on – see page 157. An explanatory leaflet **IS20** (earlier leaflet **IS1** is now obsolete) is available at post offices or from the Benefits Agency.

Working Families' Tax Credit

This has now replaced Family Credit. If you work for 16 hours a week or more, have dependent children and your savings total less than £8,000, you can apply for Working Families' Tax Credit if your weekly income is below a certain amount. How much you will receive depends on the number and age of your children and your income – see pages 156–7. Working Families' Tax Credit includes an allowance for child care for those who qualify for it. Details can be found in the explanatory leaflet **WFTC6**, supplied as a pack which includes all necessary claim forms. Forms are available from the Benefits Agency or post offices.

Housing Benefit

If your savings are less than £16,000 you may be able to claim Housing Benefit to help you pay your rent and Council Tax if your income is below a certain amount, which varies according to your circumstances. Claim forms and information are available from Local Authority offices. Leaflets **GL16**, **GL17** and **WWB5** are helpful, and booklet **RR2** contains full information. All these are obtainable from the Benefits Agency.

Industrial Injuries Disablement Benefit

If your spouse did not meet or fully meet the National Insurance contributions conditions, they may be treated as satisfied if his or her death was caused by an industrial accident or disease. For further details, see leaflet **NI6** and **NI2**.

Jobseeker's Allowance

If you are unemployed and able to look for work you may be eligible to receive Jobseeker's Allowance. This benefit replaced Unemployment Benefit and Income Support for the unemployed (except under certain circumstances) from 7 October 1996. If enough National Insurance contributions have been paid, you may be able to get contribution-based Jobseeker's Allowance; if not, you may be eligible for income-based Jobseeker's Allowance – see page 158. For further information, see leaflet **JSAL5**, available from the Benefits Agency or Jobcentre.

Guardian's Allowance

A person who takes an orphaned child into the family may be entitled to a Guardian's Allowance – see page 158. Although the payment is called a Guardian's Allowance, it is not necessary to assume legal guardianship to qualify. Usually the allowance is paid only when both parents are dead, but it can sometimes be paid after the death of one parent – for instance, where the other is missing or cannot be traced, or where the parents were divorced and the other is neither maintaining the child nor subject to any liability for maintenance. The allowance is not awarded unless one of the child's parents was a British subject or had been resident in the UK for a specified length of time. It is paid only if the guardian qualifies for child benefit for the child.

Further information is contained in leaflet **NI14,** and claims for the allowance should be made on Form **BG1**; both are obtainable from the Benefits Agency. A claim should be submitted as soon as possible after a child joins the family, otherwise some benefit may be lost.

When there is no one to take charge of a child, the local authority Social Services department should be told; it will then assume responsibility for the child. When this happens, children of the same family are kept together if at all possible.

Home Responsibilities Protection

Someone who is looking after a child or a sick or disabled person, and either does not work at all or works but does not pay enough National Insurance contributions in a tax year to make that year count for Retirement Pension purposes may benefit from Home Responsibilities Protection. This is a special arrangement which helps to protect basic Retirement Pensions.

Home Responsibilities Protection is awarded provided the qualifying conditions are satisfied, and works by reducing the number of qualifying years needed for a basic pension. For further information see Form **CF411** *Looking After Someone At Home*.

National Insurance benefits: amounts

The 1999–2000 weekly amounts payable for the benefits described in the preceding pages are as follows. DSS leaflet **GL23** should be consulted for relevant updates.

Widow's benefit

widow's payment	£1,000
widow's full-rate pension	£66.75
widowed mother's allowance	£66.75
plus for the oldest child who qualifies	£9.90
plus for each other child	£11.35

Working Families' Tax Credit

To qualify for Working Families' Tax Credit you must be a married couple, a lone parent, or a man and woman living together as if they were married. One of the couple or the lone parent must work for at least 16 hours a week, be responsible for at least one child under 16 (or under 19 if still in full-time education), and not have more than £8,000 in total savings. Each child in the household is allowed up to £2,500 in savings before Tax Credit starts to be reduced.

The maximum amount of Working Families' Tax Credit is payable if your net income is £90 a week or less. If it is more than £90, 55p will be deducted for every £1 above the basic £90. The maximum amounts payable are:

one adult credit (only one per household even if there are 2 adults)	£52.30
plus one credit for one parent working 39 hours or more	£11.05

plus a credit for each child according to age:

from birth to 11 years	£19.85
from the first Tuesday in the September following 11th birthday	£20.90
from the first Tuesday in the September following 16th birthday (if still in full-time education)	£25.95

Payment is made 2 weeks in arrears if paid direct into a bank or building society, or one week in arrears if paid by order book at a post office.

Income Support

The weekly *personal allowances* are:

aged under 18 (usual rate if eligible)	£30.95
aged under 18 (in special circumstances, if eligible)	£40.70
aged 18 to 24	£40.70
aged 25 or over	£51.40
couple (both aged 18 or over)	£80.45

Where one or both partners are aged under 18, their personal allowance will depend on their situation:

lone parents aged 16 to 17	£30.95
lone parents aged 16 to 17 in special circumstances	£40.70
lone parents aged 18 and over	£51.40

plus for each dependent child aged 11, 16 or 18 on or after 7 April 1997:

birth up to September following 11th birthday	£20.20
then up to September following 16th birthday	£25.90
then until day before 19th birthday	£30.95

The *premiums* are:

	Single	Couple
family		£13.90
lone parent	£15.75	
pensioner	£23.60	£35.95
enhanced pensioner (aged 75 to 79)	£25.90	£39.20
higher pensioner*	£30.85	£44.65
disability	£21.90	£31.25
severe disability: for each adult	£39.75	
disabled child	£21.90	
carers	£13.95	

*Aged over 80, *or* who received Disability Premium within 8 weeks of 60th birthday, *or* aged over 60 and receiving any one of Attendance Allowance, Disability Living Allowance, long-term Incapacity Benefit, Severe Disablement Allowance, *or* are registered blind or provided with an invalid vehicle.

Guardian's Allowance

for the oldest child who qualifies	£7.30
for each other child who qualifies	£11.35

Jobseeker's Allowance

Contribution-based Jobseeker's Allowance:

person aged 16 to 17	£30.95
person aged 18 to 24	£40.70
person aged 25 or over	£51.40

Income-based Jobseeker's Allowance:

Personal Allowances and Premiums follow the general pattern of payments as made for Income Support; for full information see leaflet **GL23**.

Application forms for grants, allowances and pensions

form	source	function
BD8	from registrar when registering a death	to apply for forms BG1 and BW1 for Social Security benefits
SF200	registrar, DSS office or funeral director	to claim payment for funeral expenses from the Social Fund
SF300	DSS offices	to claim loans and Community Care grants from the Social Fund
BW1	DSS offices	to claim Widow's Benefit
BG1	DSS offices	to claim Guardian's Allowance
WFTC1	Inland Revenue or DSS offices	to claim Working Families' Tax Credit
NI105	DSS offices	to apply for payment of benefit direct into banks or building societies

Leaflets available from the Benefits Agency

D49	What to do after a death in England and Wales *or* What to do after a death in Scotland
IS20	Income support
NP45	A guide to widow's benefits
NP46	Retirement pensions
RM2	Approaching retirement?
RM3	Retired?
RR2	Housing Benefit and Council Tax Benefit
BAL4	Establishing your identity for Social Security
GL16	Help with your rent
GL17	Help with your council tax

GL23	Social Security benefit rates
CH11	Child Benefit for lone parents
NI14	Guardian's Allowance
BG1	Claim for Guardian's Allowance
NI105	Retirement pension or Widow's Benefit paid straight into an account
CF411	Home Responsibilities Protection
JSAL5	Jobseeker's Allowance
WFTC6	Working Families' Tax Credit
BW1	Widow's Benefit
SB16	Guide to the Social Fund
SF200	Funeral payment from the Social Fund
SF300	Community care grants from the Social Fund
CA02	NI contributions for the self-employed with small earnings
CA04	NI contributions: direct debit
CA08	NI contributions: voluntary contributions
CA09	NI contributions for widows
WWB5	Extra help with rent and council tax

Leaflets available from Job Centres

JSAL4	Jobseeker's Allowance: part-time education and training
JSAL5	Jobseeker's Allowance
ISAL8	Jobseeker's Allowance: Income Support if you are 16 or I 7
JSAL9	Jobseeker's Allowance: Hardship provision

Leaflets available from tax offices

IR91	A guide for widows and widowers
IR45	What to do about tax when someone dies

The government, the DSS and the Inland Revenue may make substantial changes to benefits and the qualifications for claiming them at very short notice. The information given here is accurate at the time of going to press, but if you are considering claiming any DSS benefit, it is very important to contact your local Benefits Agency office as soon as possible in order to get accurate information about the current situation. Always make sure that you have the latest edition of any leaflet, and ask if anything in it has changed since it was published. You may lose some benefits if you do not do this.

Chapter 22

Before your own death

A printed form, *Instructions for my next of kin and executors upon my death*, is available from Age Concern England⋆ on receipt of a stamped, addressed envelope. Multiple copies can be obtained for 25p each. On this, you can put down details of yourself that may be useful when your death is being registered (such as your place of birth, NHS number, details of parents and spouse/s), and information about your possessions, insurance policies and employer, with spaces for the names and addresses of relevant people such as solicitor, bank manager, accountant and tax inspector. You can say on it where you keep important documents, not only your will, but birth certificate, marriage certificate, deeds of house, certificates, savings account books. Your wishes regarding your funeral can also be recorded on the form. Some funeral directors will also provide a free Personal Record File or similar document.

Make sure that your family or whoever you live with, or your executors, know about such forms and where they are kept.

The Age Concern form and others similar are not intended to take the place of a will; you are strongly advised to make a will even if you do not own very much.

The property of a person who dies intestate (that is, without leaving a valid will) is divided among the family according to the intestacy rules; if he or she has no close relatives, it may all go to the Crown.

Wills and Probate, available from Which? Books,⋆ explains how to make a will, what to say in it, how to have it witnessed, and what happens if there is no will.

It is quite customary to put into a will whether you wish your body to be cremated or buried, but it is important to let your family know because there may be a delay before the will is read.

Making your wishes about organ donation known

You should ensure that all relevant parties are aware of your intentions.

The donor card

Anyone who would like any part of his or her body to be used to save or prolong someone's life should have their name entered on the NHS Organ Donor Register (see pages 31–2). This can be done by contacting the NHS Organ Donor Registration Service★ or completing one of the small red and blue donor cards available at GPs' surgeries, hospitals, clinics, dispensing chemists, libraries and other public offices. This card should be carried with you at all times. It is important, however, to discuss your wishes with your nearest kin and your GP and let them know that you have signed a donor card as evidence of your willingness to let parts of your body be used for the treatment of others. If you go into hospital as an in-patient, be sure to tell the ward sister or other senior members of staff that you are a potential donor.

Eyes

Corneal donation alone can be considered when someone dies at home or in hospital after any illness. In this case it is important to let the GP or hospital know about the person's intention.

If you specifically want the cornea of your eyes to be used, you can get in touch with the prevention of blindness services co-ordinator at the Royal National Institute for the Blind (RNIB).★ You will be sent a multi-organ donor card to sign and keep, a leaflet giving information on what is involved, and a letter with details of the appropriate hospital to be contacted in your area.

The body

Before expressing a formal wish that your whole body be used for anatomical examination and medical education, you should discuss the matter with your family and next of kin, and also tell your executors, because they will have to act quickly after you have died.

To make the arrangements, you should contact the professor of anatomy at your nearest medical school or HM Inspector of Anatomy★ at the Department of Health. In Scotland the Scottish Office Department of Health★ can provide information.

For information about brain donation, see page 34.

Requesting cremation

People who wish to be cremated could register with the Cremation Society* under a scheme called FATE (Funeral Arrangements for Trustees and Executors). This scheme has now been suspended, and no new names are being registered. Those who have registered, however, should be assured that all arrangements that have been made previously will be carried out.

The majority of funerals now involve cremation, and most people make their relatives aware of their wishes in this respect. A note to executors or family on a plain piece of paper is quite valid, although even if you leave specific instructions that you want – or do not want – your body to be cremated, there is no legal obligation on executors or next of kin to carry out your wishes. If you do leave written instructions for friends or family, make sure that they know where the instructions are to be found.

Pre-payment for the funeral

Pre-payment plans for funerals, which are big business in the USA, are now very heavily marketed in Britain, particularly on daytime television. It may not benefit you financially as an individual to pay in advance for your funeral, and you may well prefer to have the cost met in the usual way (see page 113), from your estate after your death, or to put the money aside in an interest-earning account. But if you are keen to ensure that your specific personal wishes regarding your funeral are carried out, or want to spare relatives and friends the task of organising and possibly paying for your funeral, you may decide to opt for a pre-paid funeral plan. A number of pre-payment schemes are currently available, all offering a selection of funeral types and prices. Almost all the schemes offer at least three choices:

- *basic*: a simple, basic funeral service which covers all the funeral director's charges and disbursements paid to crematoria, minister, doctors etc. Such plans usually specify cremation, but can be changed to burial, which may involve an extra charge (burial is normally more expensive than cremation)
- *standard*: the funeral director's 'normal' service, as above, but including a better-quality coffin, a limousine for mourners, disbursements covering either burial or cremation, and often other services

- *superior*: a service as above but including a solid wood coffin, two or more limousines for mourners, all disbursements and other services.

A recent scheme allows the client to choose a tailor-made funeral, specifying all the details. Most schemes now make a qualified commitment to honour the disbursements, making the reservation that extra charges may be made if the cost of disbursements (cremation or burial fee, and so on) rises above the rate of inflation.

These plans are marketed under various names, according to the organisation which provides them. Normally, funeral directors are agents for only one scheme (which will include at least the three categories above), and several sources should be investigated before a choice is made. There are currently at least five different schemes available in the UK, one of which is organised by the National Association of Funeral Directors.★ Leaflets and brochures explaining all the schemes are available from funeral directors, or by response to advertisements in the media. Clients should ensure that the company promoting the chosen scheme has a nationally known trust fund (such as a high street bank or equivalent) into which fees are paid, so that all money set aside for funeral payments is protected. They should further ensure that the chosen scheme is a member of the National Association for Pre-paid Funeral Plans (NAPFP)★ or the Funeral Planning Council (FPC).★

Payment is made either by a lump sum or by instalments. The lump-sum payment for the cheapest version of all the schemes currently on offer is in the region of £900 (2000), and should cover the total cost of the funeral, no matter how much prices may rise. Instalments are payable over a number of years, which vary according to the scheme chosen. Should death occur before instalments are fully paid, a sum equal to the number of instalments due will need to be paid by the executors. Proceeds are paid into a trust fund administered by independent, reputable authorities.

It is normal for a funeral director (not necessarily the one consulted) to be chosen at the time of taking out the plan; when death occurs, the central office of the company promoting the plan is informed, which then instructs the funeral director to carry out the funeral arrangements.

Addresses

Many organisations exist to offer help and support to bereaved individuals and families. Details of some are provided below, along with those of other organisations mentioned in the text.

Age Concern England
Astral House, 1268 London Road
Norbury, London SW16 4ER
Tel: 020-8679 8000
Fax: 020-8765 7211
Email: infodep@ace.org.uk
Web site: www.ace.org.uk

Age Concern Northern Ireland
3 Lower Crescent
Belfast BT7 1NR
Tel: 028-9024 5729
Fax: 028-9023 5497
Email: ageconcern.ni@
btinternet.com

Age Concern Scotland
113 Rose Street
Edinburgh EH2 3DT
Tel: 0131-220 3345
Fax: 0131-220 2779
Email: enquiries@acsinfo3.
freeserve.co.uk

Age Concern Wales
4th Floor, 1 Cathedral Road
Cardiff CF11 9SD
Tel: 029-2037 1566
Fax: 029-2039 9562
Email: accymru@ace.org.uk
Web site: www.accymru.org.uk

Age Concern Funeral Plan
Tel: (0800) 387718 (*freephone*)

Asian Funeral Service
209 Kenton Road, Harrow
Middlesex HA3 0HD
Tel: 020-8909 3737
Fax: 020-8909 3435
Email: asianfuneralservice@
btinternet.com

Association of Burial Authorities
Waterloo House
155 Upper Street
London N1 1RA
Tel: 020-7288 2522
Fax: 020-7288 2533
Email: aba@swa-pr.co.uk
Web site: www.swa-pr.co.uk

Association of Charity Officers
Beechwood House
Wyllyotts Close
Potters Bar EN6 2HN
Tel: (01707) 651777
Fax: (01707) 660477

Benefits Agency
Look in your local phone book

British Humanist Association
47 Theobalds Road
London WC1X 8SP
Tel: 020-7430 0908
Fax: 020-7430 1271
Email: robert@humanism.org.uk
Web site: www.humanism.org.uk

British Organ Donors Society (BODY)
Balsham
Cambridge CB1 6DL
Tel/Fax: (01223) 893636 (*call before sending fax*)
Email: body@argonet.co.uk
Web site: www.argonet.co.uk/body

Citizens Advice Bureau
Look in your local phone book

Compassionate Friends
53 North Street
Bristol BS3 1EN
Tel: 0117-966 5202
0117-953 9639 (*helpline*)
Fax: 0117-914 4368
Email: info@tcf.org.uk
Web site: www.tcf.org.uk

Cremation Society
2nd Floor, Brecon House
16–16a Albion Place
Maidstone ME14 5DZ
Tel: (01622) 688292/3
Fax: (01622) 686698
Email: cremsoc@aol.com
Web site: www.cremation.org.uk

Cruse: Bereavement Care
Cruse House, 126 Sheen Road
Richmond TW9 1UR
Tel: 020-8940 4818
(0345) 585565 (*counselling line*)
020-8332 7227 (*local information*)
Fax: 020-8940 7638
Send SAE for free leaflets

Driver and Vehicle Licensing Agency (DVLA)
Swansea SA1 1AA
Tel: (01792) 772151
Web site: www.open.gov.uk/dvla

Foreign and Commonwealth Office
Consular Division
Nationality and Passport Section

Room 3.3.17
1 Palace Street
London SW1E 5HE
Tel: 020-7238 4567
(*9.30a.m.–12.30p.m.*)
Fax: 020-7238 4557

Foundation for the Study of Infant Deaths (FSID)
14 Halkin Street
London SW1X 7DP
Tel: 020-7235 0965
020-7235 1721 (*24-hour helpline*)
Fax: 020-7823 1986
Email: fsid@sids.org.uk
Web site: www.sids.org.uk/fsid/

Funeral Ombudsman Scheme
26–28 Bedford Row
London WC1R 4HE
Tel: 020-7430 1112
Fax: 020-7430 1012
Email: fos@dircon.co.uk

Funeral Planning Council (FPC)
Melville House
70 Drymen Road
Bearsden, Glasgow G61 2RP
Tel: 0141-942 5855
Fax: 0141-942 2323

Funeral Standards Council (FSC)
30 North Road
Cardiff CF1 3DY
Tel: 029-2038 2046
Fax: 029-2022 0827

General Register Office
Smedley Hydro
Trafalgar Road, Birkdale
Merseyside PR8 2HH
Tel: (01704) 569824
Fax: (01704 568315
(01704) 550013 (*certificate*)
Email: certificates.services@
ons.gov.uk
Web site: www.ons.gov.uk

General Register Office for Scotland
New Register House
3 West Register Street
Edinburgh EH1 3YT
Tel: 0131-334 0380
Fax: 0131-314 4400
Email: gros@gtnet.gov.uk
Web site: www.open.gov.uk/gros/
groshome.htm

HM Inspector of Anatomy
Room 614, Department of Health
Wellington House
135–155 Waterloo Road
London SE1 8UG
Tel: 020-7972 4551
Fax: 020-7972 4791
Email: khuscrof@doh.gov.uk

Home Office
Constitution and Community Policy
Unit Directorate
Room 972, Coroner's Section
Queen Anne's Gate
London SW1H 9AT
Tel: 020-7273 3776
Fax: 020-7273 4231
Email: bevan.hinds@
homeoffice.ssi.gov.uk
Web site: gem.ho@gmet.gov.uk

INQUEST
Ground Floor
Alexandra National House
330 Seven Sisters Road
London N4 2PJ
Tel: 020-8802 7430
Fax: 020-8802 7450
Email: info@inquest.freeserve.co.uk
Web site: www.gn.apc.org/inquest/

Institute of Family Therapy
24–32 Stephenson Way
London NW1 2HX
Tel: 020-7391 9150
Fax: 020-7391 9169
Email: ift@psyc.bbk.ac.uk

**Iris Fund for the Prevention of
Blindness**
2nd Floor, York House
199 Westminster Bridge Road
London SE1 7UT
Tel: 020-7928 7743
Fax: 020-7928 7919
Email: ron@irisfund.org.uk
Web site: irisfund.org.uk

**Jewish Bereavement Counselling
Service**
PO Box 6748
London N3 3BX
Tel/Fax: 020-8349 0839

Law Society
Look in your local phone book

Lesbian and Gay Bereavement Project
Vaughan Williams Centre
Colindale Hospital
London NW9 5HG
Tel: 020-8200 0511
Helpline: 020-8455 8894
(7p.m.–10.30p.m.)
Fax: 020-8200 1345

London Bereavement Network
356 Holloway Road
London N7 6PA
Tel: 020-7700 8134
Fax: 020-7700 8146
Email: info@bereavement.org.uk
Web site: www.bereavement.org.uk

London Regional Transport
55 Broadway
London SW1H 0BD
Tel: 020-7918 4300
Fax: 020-7918 3999
Email:
enquire@londontransport.co.uk
Web site:
www.londontransport.co.uk

Macmillan Cancer Relief Fund
15–19 Britten Street
London SW3 3BR
Tel: 020-7351 7811
(0845) 6016161 (*information line*)
Fax: 020-7376 8098
Web site: www.macmillan.org.uk

Miscarriage Association
c/o Clayton Hospital
Northgate, Wakefield
West Yorkshire WF1 3JS
Tel: (01924) 200799
Fax: (01924) 298834
Email: susan.ellis@btinternet.com
Web site: www.btinternet.com/
~miscarriageassociation

**National Association of Funeral
Directors (NAFD)**
618 Warwick Road
Solihull
West Midlands B91 1AA
Tel: 0121-711 1343
Fax: 0121-711 1351
Email: info@nafd.org.uk
Web site: www.nafd.org.uk

**National Association of Memorial
Masons**
27a Albert Street, Rugby
Warwickshire CV21 2SG
Tel: (01788) 542264
Fax: (01788) 542276
Email: enquiries@namm.org.uk
Web site: www.namm.org.uk

**National Association for Pre-paid
Funeral Plans**
618 Warwick Road, Solihull
West Midlands B91 1AA
Tel: 0121-711 1343
Fax: 0121-711 1351

National Association of Widows
54–57 Allison Street
Digbeth
Birmingham B5 5TH

Tel: 0121-643 8348
Email: wat@dial.pipex.com

**National Council for Voluntary
Organisations**
Regents Wharf
8 All Saints Street
London N1 9RL
Tel: 020-7713 6161
Fax: 020-7713 6300
Email: ncvo@ncvo-vol.org.uk
Web site: www.ncvo-vol.org.uk

National Secular Society
25 Red Lion Square
London WC1R 4RL
Tel/Fax: 020-7404 3126
Email: kpw@secularism.org.uk
Web site: www.secularism.org.uk

Natural Death Centre
20 Heber Road
London NW2 6AA
Tel: 020-8208 2853
Fax: 020-8452 6434
Email: rhino@dial.pipex.com
Web site: www.globalideasbank.org/
naturaldeath.html

NHS Organ Donor Register
UK Transplant Support Service
Authority
Foxden Road, Stoke Gifford
Bristol BS34 8RR
Tel: 0117-975 7575
Fax: 0117-975 7577
*The register deals with previously registered
donors*

**NHS Organ Donor Registration
Service**
PO Box 14
FREEPOST
Patchway, Bristol BS34 8ZZ
Tel: (0845) 606 0400 (*information line*)
*Contact the service to register as an organ
donor*

Overseas Branch of the Department of Social Security
Benefits Agency
Tyneview Park, Whitley Road
Benton, Newcastle-upon-Tyne
NE12 9SG
Tel: 0191-213 5000
Fax: *call for relevant number*
Email: baadmin@baadmin.
demon.co.uk
Web site: www.dss.gov.uk/ba

Parkinsons Disease Society of the UK
215 Vauxhall Bridge Road
London SW1V 1EJ
Tel: 020-7931 8080
Helpline: (0808) 8000303
(*Mon–Fri 9.30a.m.–5.30p.m.*)
Fax: 020-7233 9226
Email: mailbox@pdsuk.demon.co.uk
Web site: www.shef.ac.uk/misc/
groups/epda/parkuk.htm

Passport Office
Clive House
70 Petty France
London SW1H 9HD
Tel: (0870) 5210410 (*enquiry line*)
Call for details of your local office

Public Search Room
Family Records Centre
1 Myddleton Street
London EC1R 1UW
Tel: 020-8392 5300
Certificate enquiries: 020-7533 9233
Fax: 020-8392 5307
Email: certificate.services@
ons.gov.uk
Web site: www.pro.gov.uk

Rationalist Press Association
Bradlaugh House
47 Theobalds Road
London WC1X 8SP
Tel: 020-7430 1371
Fax: 020-7430 1271

Email: info@humanism.org.uk
Web site: www.humanism.org.uk

Registrar General (Northern Ireland)
Oxford House
49–55 Chichester Street
Belfast BT1 4HH
Tel: 028-9025 2163
(*9.30a.m.–4.00p.m.*)
028-9025 2029 (*credit-card line*)
Fax: 028-9025 2044
Web site: www.nisra.gov.uk/gro/

Registry of Shipping and Seamen
PO Box 165
Cardiff CF14 5FU
Tel: 029-2076 8227
Fax: 029-2074 7877
Email: rss@mcga.gov.uk

Roadpeace
PO Box 2579
London NW10 3PW
Tel/Fax: 020-838 5102
020-8964 1021(*support line*)
Email: info@roadpeace.org.uk
Web site: www.roadpeace.org.uk
Support and information for those bereaved by road death

Royal National Institute for the Blind (RNIB)
224 Great Portland Street
London W1N 6AA
Tel: 020-7388 1266
(08457) 669999 (*helpline*)
Fax: 020-7388 2034
Email: rnib@rnib.org.uk
Web site: www.rnib.org.uk

Samaritans
Head Office
10 The Grove, Slough
Berkshire SL1 1QP
Tel: (01753) 216500
Helpline: (0345) 909090 (*24-hr*)
Fax: (01753) 819004
Email: jo@samaritans.org.uk

Web site: www.samaritans.org.uk
Look in your telephone book for local branch

Scottish Office Department of Health
St Andrews House
Regent Road
Edinburgh EH1 3DG
Tel: 0131–556 8400
Fax: *call for relevant number*
Web site: www.scotland.gov.uk

Sea Fisheries Inspectorate
Ministry of Agriculture
Room 515, Nobel House
17 Smith Square
London SW1P 3JR
Tel: 020–7238 5815
Fax: 020–7238 5814
Email: sfiadmin@fish.gov.uk
Web site: www.maff.gov.uk

Society of Allied and Independent Funeral Directors (SAIF)
3 Bullfields, Sawbridgeworth
Hertfordshire CM21 9DB
Tel: (01279) 726777
Fax: (01279) 726300
Email: info@saif.org.uk
Web site: www.saif.org.uk

South Place Ethical Society
Conway Hall
25 Red Lion Square
London WC1R 4RL
Tel: 020–7242 8037
Fax: 020–7242 8036

Stillbirth and Neonatal Death Society (SANDS)
28 Portland Place
London W1N 4DE
Tel: 020–7436 7940
020–7436 5881 (*helpline*)
Fax: 020–7436 3715

Support after Murder and Manslaughter (SAMM)
Cranmer House
39 Brixton Road
London SW9 6DZ
Tel: 020–7735 3838
Fax: 020–7735 3900
Email: samm@ukpeople.net

UK Transplant Support Service Authority (UKTSSA)
Information Executive
Foxden Road
Stoke Gifford
Bristol BS34 8RR
Written enquiries only

War Pensions Agency
Norcross
Blackpool FY5 3WP
Tel: (01253) 858858 (*helpline*)
Fax: (01253) 333737
Email: warpensions@gtnet.gov.uk
Web site:
www.dss.gov.uk/wpa/index.htm

Which? Books
PO Box 44
Hertford X, SG14 1LH
Tel: (0800) 252100
Fax: (0800) 533053
Web site: www.which.net

Index